LIVING IN LOVE AND JUSTICE

Colin Brown

A STUDY GUIDE ON CHRISTIAN ETHICS

Illustrations by Dan Simonds

Published by
The Baptist Union of Great Britain
April 1995

Designed, typeset and produced for the Baptist Union of Great Britain by
Gem Publishing Company, Brightwell, Wallingford, Oxfordshire.
Printed in Great Britain by Swindon Press Limited, Swindon.

CONTENTS

Acknowledgements

I wish to thank all those students past and present, and friends who have both help shape my ideas. My particular thanks to all those people who have kindly read drafts of this work book and that let me have benefit of their wise counsel.

Introduction

This is a book to help you think about the decisions most of us have to make about what is morally right and morally wrong. That is an important matter in the life of most of us, because they are the kind of decisions that can have a major effect on our lives. An obvious example is the way in which people may decide what is the morally right thing to do when they are wondering whether to divorce their partner. Again, moral considerations may affect the decision a woman will take about having an abortion. Ethics can have far-reaching effects upon our lives.

Sometimes our decisions are based on attitudes and beliefs that are almost part of us, and we do not have to think about them. We gain them from a variety of influences upon us. Our morality is something we learn from our earliest times as our parents teach us and our friends influence us. The society in which we live shapes our views and if we are members of a church, our views are likely to be further refined, and maybe even revolutionised, by what we learn there. Yet there are times when we have to consciously decide what we ought or ought not do or think or say. For example, as medical science advances it presents us with a series of new moral problems and the need to at least form a general view of their moral standing. There are also occasions when we may find that our long cherished moral views are challenged by new and unusual situations, and we may wonder if we ought to have a rethink, and question whether our previous views were really as clear as we thought.

Although it is tempting to think that there is a Christian answer to moral problems, listening to what Christians say and reading what they write suggests that over some issues there are quite profound disagreements between them – yet they would all claim that their position reflects Christian values. As we will see, there are reasons why such disagreements are understandable. In this book we will be exploring some of the ways in which Christians make their decisions, and we will try to understand why they sometimes disagree and what things ought to be common to them all in their search to know what is right and wrong.

In the first three units we will look at some ways in which we make our decisions about what is right and wrong. Then in Units 4 to 8 we look at a Christian way of taking decisions that seeks to do justice, both to the biblical records and to the ways in which we often proceed. In Unit 9 we will look at those difficult cases where decisions are not easy, and finally, in Units 10 to 12, we will see how the way in which we take our decisions is worked out in coming to the view we take about punishment, euthanasia and cohabitation.

As we try to understand some of the factors that form Christian approaches to moral questions, you will be invited to pause in your reading and to think, and maybe write down your ideas about various things. Sometimes you may find it helpful to talk over some of the ideas you will meet with another person. These invitations are like exercises which are intended to help you clarify your own ideas, and as such they are an important part of your study. You may find it helpful to get a notebook and write down all your answers, but at least try to think about the matters that we will be considering.

ACTIVITY

Write down the names of those who have helped you form your ideas of right and wrong and, if you can, say what you now believe you learnt from them.

PART 1
SETTING THE SCENE

Unit 1 HOW DO WE DECIDE?

OBJECTIVES

When you have completed this unit you should be able to:

- *Understand some of the factors that influence our moral decision making*

- *Appreciate the diversity of ways in which people make moral decisions.*

At various times in our lives we have to take decisions about what is the morally right thing to do. On some occasions we are faced with situations where we have to decide whether it is right for us to do something or not. At other times we are not directly involved but we hear or read of events and if we form an attitude to them, it often involves an opinion about what is right and wrong. Sometimes these decisions and attitudes relate to issues that arise in matters that are of great importance to us, often affecting questions of birth or death, of relationships or the way we live together in society.

Whatever the issues though, Christian ethics is not only about the decisions we take. It is also concerned with the way we come to our decisions, and the reasons for them. The *way in which we arrive* at our decisions is important, because it is our approach and the moral awareness we possess that enable us to face new situations and make new decisions. To help us understand what may be involved in forming this awareness, let us think of the situations faced by three people.

JOHN

John is a conscientious man who believes that it is morally unacceptable to break the law, but let us suppose that one day he is driving in the middle lane of a crowded motorway, and realises that although the speed limit is 70 mph, inadvertently he is in a stream of traffic that is moving at 80 mph, and so quite unintentionally he is breaking the law. As much as he would like to, he cannot slow down, and in this situation he realises that to try to move into the slower nearside lane would be dangerous, and in the interests of safety he feels he has no choice but to continue at the same speed. The problem is that John feels some guilt as he recognises that he is legally, and in his view morally, in the wrong.

Although John is breaking the laws of the country, and that is not necessarily the same as breaking a moral law, his situation raises some interesting insights into the way we make our moral decisions. For example, John has a conscience about law-breaking and works on the principle that his conscience is an inbuilt guide to what is right and wrong – whether that is in legal matters such as speeding or more obviously moral actions like truth telling. John is not alone in this, for many of us use our conscience as one of the guides that help us decide between right and wrong.

However, John can ease his conscience because although he knows he is breaking the law, that is certainly not his intention, and when the opportunity arises he will move into the inside lane and bring his speed down to 70 mph. If John set out to do something we believe is for the benefit of someone, and it goes wrong in some way and becomes something that causes hurt and damage, we are likely to be sympathetic and not be quick to apportion blame, because it is important to us that 'he meant well'. It is experiences such as this that have led John to hold the view that we should decide what is right and wrong by looking at our intentions, and John is not alone in holding such a view.

John's situation is of interest in another way. When we think about his situation, we may wonder if his *particular situation changes what is right and wrong*. Let us suppose that on an open road with few cars in sight, he would keep to the speed limit and accept that it would be quite wrong of him to exceed the limit. But we might argue that his present situation changes what counts as right and wrong and that

"BUT HE MEANT WELL"

what is wrong when there is only a little traffic, is acceptable in the situation he now finds himself in.

It may seem strange to think in this way, but the fact is that John cannot do anything about the situation, so we really ought not to apportion blame. After all, he is not responsible for his actions when hemmed in by a lot of traffic.

This is the general principle that is sometimes applied by the courts when, for example, they accept that a person is not to be held guilty because he or she is of diminished responsibility. Implicit in such a decision is the fact that the accused is incapable of deciding whether an action is right or wrong. Wise parents take this into account when young children misbehave, and one of the questions we ask of very young offenders is, 'Does he know the difference between right and wrong?' In other words, can he choose to behave in other ways? Is he responsible for his actions?

John's situation was apparently uncomplicated, yet it raises a number of issues when we begin to ask questions about the morality of exceeding the speed limit, not least of which is the role of our intentions. Sophie faced a situation that interests ethicists in other ways.

SOPHIE

Sophie is a daughter of one of the deacons of her local church and as a result of being raped, she has now discovered that she is pregnant. She is in considerable distress because the circumstances of the conception mean that she finds it hard to even contemplate carrying the foetus to full term, yet she has been taught that abortion is always morally wrong. This belief is part of the tradition of her particular branch of Christianity, which is an important part of her life. But it is not *just* a matter of tradition. Sophie can also give some reasons for her views on abortion. She believes that the worth of an individual is present from the moment of conception, and abortion is always the taking of a life; hence it is always morally wrong and against the will of God.

The other factor that makes Sophie interesting for ethicists is that she has a view of morality that is about having a set of clearly-specified rules about right and wrong, and abiding by them, even to the point where her friends sometimes think she is legalistic in her approach. One of her rules is that God must be obeyed at all times, whilst another is that the taking of life is against the will of God. The result is that abortion is morally wrong.

She finds that in general this rule-governed way of doing ethics is clear and precise and gives her a sense of security in that it enables her to know right from wrong. There are times though when she reads about new advances in medical science and is aware that she does not have a rule for each and every event that may happen.

We may agree with Sophie that abortion is a morally wrong thing to do, but as with John, we are faced with the possibility that her particular circumstances give us good grounds for saying that in this case abortion is a morally acceptable thing to do. Once again we have an example of a complicated situation where we may want to take account of more than our basic belief about the rightness of a particular action.

This is what is causing Sophie so much concern. Her emotions are mixed because the circumstances of her conception mean she dreads having to carry the foetus to full term – indeed, her doctor believes that she could have a breakdown if she is forced to do so. She cannot believe that is right. Yet she cannot believe it is right to have an abortion. The limitations of her rules are all too apparent in her present situation.

DANA

Dana faces a situation that raises a different set of questions. She lives in a country ruled by a brutal regime which she hates and would dearly like to see replaced by a more humanitarian government which respects the rights of ordinary people. One day she finds out that in her town there are some agents of an underground movement committed to just such a government, and she does what she can to help them. Unfortunately the secret police become suspicious and accuse her of aiding enemies of the state. She is tortured in an attempt to find out where the agents are hiding, and in the interests of the future of her country, she lies and denies knowing anything about them.

Dana has been brought up to believe that telling lies is morally wrong, yet she faces a dilemma because she also believes that men and women should be treated with dignity and that we all have obligations to treat one another as we would like to be treated. In other words, she faces a conflict in that if she takes one line of action she will be unable to take the other – yet both are of equal importance to her.

Dana's problem is not unusual. An idea such as "telling lies is morally wrong" generally finds agreement in Western society, and suggests that moral issues are simple. But quite often we face moral dilemmas because the situations with which we have to live are complex and present us with difficulties about what we take to be right and wrong. For example, we may believe that stealing is wrong, but if we have children who will die unless they receive food for which we cannot pay, we may believe that stealing food becomes justified. Stealing may be morally wrong, but then so is letting a child die of hunger when food is available. A similar dilemma occurs when the doctor of a person who is terminally ill tells the patient a lie about his or her condition. He may well believe that lying is morally wrong but then it is also wrong to cause distress to men and women in that situation.

For Dana, the justification of her action is to be found in its consequences, which she believes to be good. She may want to go so far as to say that *the good of the majority* is what should decide moral matters, and that is a point of view that has a long and distinguished history. Sometimes it is expressed in the view that we should seek the greatest good of the greatest number.

As with John, we are faced with the possibility that the situation may be a reason for changing what we count as right and wrong. One of the charges that can be laid against Dana is that she assumes that bad government justifies the telling of lies, and that is to say that the end justifies the means. Yet there are cases where we are positively drawn to such a view, as for example when someone sacrifices their own life so that others may live. But there are other cases where we may want to question that the ends justify the means. For example, where a good end such as the harmony of a nation is achieved by the subjection of a minority within it, we may wish to question such a means to the end. Similarly, some would claim that if economic growth and a high standard of living can only be achieved at the cost of high unemployment, then the price is unacceptable.

"THE LESSER OF TWO EVILS?"

Despite the problems though, Dana's situation may well make us wonder if there are not some cases where we can agree that some undesirable means *are* justified by the ends. In Dana's case the question can be posed another way. She could legitimately ask: Is the evil of telling a lie *outweighed* by the evils of a totalitarian dictatorship? Like many of us, if she stopped and thought about things, she would have to decide which was the lesser of two evils.

The major issue that Dana's behaviour raises for our purposes, is the extent to which *ends* have a place in the way in which she decides on what is morally right and wrong. For Dana they certainly do have a place, but what should that place be?

ACTIVITY

Before you go further, take some time to think about the following story and, in the same way that we considered John, Sophie and Dana, try to identify some of the possible considerations in looking at the morality of this event. Try to write down why you think that it is either morally right or morally wrong.

Ben's marriage to Martha is in danger of failing because of Martha's childlessness. Both of them have been tested, and they have been told that Ben is infertile, a fact that he refuses to accept. Martha believes that the only way to avoid a divorce is for her to have a child, and it is with the desire to save the marriage that she approaches her brother-in-law, James, and after explaining the situation, suggests that he fathers her child whilst letting Ben believe it is his child. James agrees and in due time Martha gives birth to a boy, with Ben believing that he is the father. He never knows the truth, but his relationship with Martha improves and the marriage is saved.

If possible, discuss these events with someone else. You may have clear views about the morality of what happened, but try to be neutral and ask yourself what issues might be involved in coming to any conclusions. Be careful to remember that in this instance you are not thinking about ways of handling the pastoral problems that may be involved, but you are trying to pick out the same kind of considerations that we thought about earlier in this unit. If you have an opinion about Martha's actions, make a note of the reasons you would give if asked to justify your views.

How then do we take our decisions? Often we just have a 'feel' that something is right or wrong, but when we stop and think about it, how do we justify what we do or don't do? What makes us think of an action as being morally right, or how do we decide that it is morally wrong? However we do it, the situations we have thought about in this unit suggest that there may be a number of factors that influence our views of what is morally right and wrong. You may be quite clear how you decide right from wrong, but on the other hand you may think that it is not as simple as at first seems to be the case.

So far there has been no mention of a Christian view of ethics, but in subsequent units we will look at a possible Christian approach to deciding moral questions, which will help us to make our decisions.

In the next two units we will begin to think about some of the matters raised by John, Sophie and Dana. We will examine some of the rules that people use to guide their moral lives, and then look at some of the problems we face when we try to build our ethics on the way we use the *consequences* of what we do as a measure of right and wrong.

Unit 2 LIVING BY THE RULES

OBJECTIVES

When you have completed this unit you should be able to:

- *Understand the role of moral rules in determining people's conduct*
- *Identify the spoken and unspoken rules which have influenced you and members of your church*
- *Survey Jesus' attitude towards rules*
- *Appreciate the historical and cultural context of rules.*

Sophie and Dana had something in common with John. They all had excellent motives. Sophie was motivated by a desire to do the right thing to respect life, Dana by a concern for the dignity of human beings with rights, and John by the need to maintain the rule of law. In Sophie's case, her motives were of secondary importance to the *rules* that governed her life. Dana, on the other hand, primarily took her decisions by thinking of the *effects* of what she did. John was different to them both. His *motives* were the measure by which he decided the morality of his actions. If his motives were good, then his actions were good.

John's position is attractive. All too often we fail to be the kind of person other people would like us to be, and it is comforting to know that we have acted with the best of intentions. It is also a position that reflects something of Jesus' teaching in the Sermon on the Mount, when he spoke of the importance of what we think as well as of what we do (Matthew 5:21–30). What we would *like* to do matters, as well as *what* we do.

However, in forming moral conduct it is difficult to separate out our motives from our actions and their consequences, because there is an intention behind the behaviour of people like Sophie and Dana. Their situations raise a problem that John has as well, namely, that of knowing what is a good motive. We may have more than one motive, some of which we are not always aware of. In theory, we may want to say that good intentions are a form of settling moral issues. In practice they leave us with the need to evaluate them in the light of other criteria, and in effect this is what Sophie and Dana did. For Dana, her intentions were related to the outcome of her actions, whilst Sophie's motive was to keep the rules on which she based her moral life.

Sophie had a number of problems. It was not just that she had been raped and had to live with the pain of that. It was not just that she found herself pregnant as a result of it, though that too was horrendous. As though these were not enough, she found it difficult to relate her situation to her moral beliefs. She had been taught a series of rules for living and in general they served her well, but her present situation raised questions in her mind about the extent to which they were applicable to her when she was torn between keeping her rules and having to cope with her situation.

If we had asked Sophie how she normally made her moral decisions and how she knew what was right and what was wrong, she would probably have said that she looked to see what her Bible had to say about the matter. In other words, she measured what is right and wrong by God's commands, and many other Christians would share her views.

Interestingly, many who do not claim to follow Christ in any other way say something similar. For them the Bible is essentially a *moral guide* and a return to moral basics means a return to the standards laid down in passages such as the Sermon on the Mount and the Ten Commandments. At various times the position of Religious Education in schools has been defended on the grounds that it teaches moral values. So Sophie is not alone in looking to the Bible for some rules that will help to direct her moral life. Later we will consider what kind of rules the Bible gives us, but for now it is the idea of there being moral rules at all that is of interest.

THE RULES WE MAKE

We are all used to rules. Children are told the school rules about running in corridors, adults know there are rules that govern the games they play or the organisations they join. We know some of the laws which govern the way our society runs and we know there are rules that govern such things as the way in which we use land, and the buildings we can put up. Rules and laws are a part of life and we know that we are behaving correctly when we

15

act in accordance with them. In many cases, right actions are those that correctly apply the appropriate rules. The same is true about our moral behaviour. Sophie had a rule that said that abortion is always wrong and for her, right behaviour meant that abortions ought never to take place.

The reason why some of the moral rules we adopt are helpful is that, like rules about stopping at traffic lights, they always apply because they assume that there is something intrinsic about some actions that makes them morally right or wrong. If we have a rule that says that we must not tell lies, we often assume it is because there is something about lying that makes it morally wrong. Similarly with stealing or child abuse. Our rules say that we should not do such things because they are intrinsically wrong. The result is that we make lists of such rules and are pleased to have them, because they give us clear moral directions.

ACTIVITY

Christians often have lists of rules even though they are often unspoken. Think about your church and see if you can identify any rules that its members are expected to follow. It may help you if you think of the things you do or want to do which you would not broadcast throughout the fellowship – not because you think they are necessarily wrong, but because your fellow Christians do not always share your views.

If our moral decisions are governed by rules, then we know what things we ought or ought not to do and being morally good means following the rules – though we have to add that there are times when we recognise that our own set of rules do not always match those held by other people, and that there are some rules which are debatable.

Some Christians claim that artificial contraception is morally wrong because it breaks a moral rule. For some Christians the drinking of alcohol may mean breaking such a rule. In both cases, other equally committed and devout Christians disagree.

But there are other rules that we may want to say apply to everyone and are non-negotiable. We may see them as the absolutes of moral life that apply to everyone, irrespective of the circumstances involved. Some Christians see the Ten Commandments in this way.

SOME DISADVANTAGES OF RULES

Perhaps when you listed your set of rules, you realised how helpful they are in giving a framework to your life, but there is also a danger that you will follow them with a legalistic frame of mind. One result may be that the rules become a burden to you rather than helping you to lead a full life. This legalistic frame of mind was a problem for the Pharisees in Jesus' day. They prescribed a complex and detailed set of rules in which they sought to cover all eventualities. As you read the gospels you may notice that the rules led them to judge people by the extent to which they obeyed them, without reference to their need.

There is a difficulty in basing our moral life on a set of rules which seek to cover the details of life, and that is of deciding which rules it is appropriate to have. We may use what seem to be biblical rules, but they were laid down at a time and in a culture that was different from our own. An example of the consequences of this is that there are many current medical practices that were unknown in biblical times, and for which we do not have specific biblical rules. How are we to agree on the rules that govern new practices?

The dilemma can be illustrated in another way. The Puritans rejected theatre-going, whilst following the Second World War many evangelical Christians believed it was wrong to enter public houses or cinemas for pleasure. Evangelical Christian women were expected not to use make-up. Rightly or wrongly, such rules do not have the force they once had, and it raises the question whether some of the rules we have used in the past reflected historical and cultural considerations that determined what we took to be a Christian life.

There is one more difficulty in this narrow rule approach. What do we do if two rules conflict? Sophie's uncertainty as to whether to have an abortion or not arises from this problem. One of the rules by which she lived said that abortion is always morally wrong, but she also implicitly believed that it was morally good to defend the quality of life – in this case, her life. Which should take precedent? Basing ethics on rules that are very specific can, at times, cause us difficulties.

Despite the difficulties these narrow rules present, they are helpful and many Christians form such rules and seek to guide their life by them. They may become legalistic and at times they may have problems in knowing what to do when facing new moral dilemmas. Nevertheless this approach gives the security of firm moral direction, and as such is helpful. In a later unit we will think about the fact that this appears to be the approach taken by the writers of the Bible.

RULES AND PRINCIPLES

There is an alternative form of rules that may be of more help to Sophie. These rules do not apply directly to specific instances but act as general principles. For example, we may want to make rules that property, life and truth-telling should be respected. Such rules are less specific than the narrower alternatives we have been thinking about. We may have a narrow rule that we return borrowed tools when their owner wants them, but the corresponding wider rule will say that we respect the property and rights of other people. One of the differences between the two types of rule is that narrow rules lay down specific behaviours whilst the wider rules give us general principles which often require that we think how they should be applied to particular situations. The result is that we may not all agree about the way they should be applied.

In their favour though, is the fact that they are far more flexible and can express the *intention* of the rule rather than its rigid application. There is an occasion in the gospel that we have already looked at, when Jesus seems to have invoked a wide rule to counter the narrow rule of the Pharisees that man should conform to the requirements of Sabbath-observance. When he was challenged about his disciples eating the ears of grain on the Sabbath, he replied, '*"The Sabbath was made for man, not man for the Sabbath"*' (Mark 2: 27). It is an appeal to the *spirit* of Sabbath-keeping rather than an inflexible application of a narrow set of rules.

These wide rules act as principles and as such give us frameworks which we can use in our moral decision-making. As such they apply across cultural differences and social change. For example, if we accept that loving our neighbour is one of the wide rules we will follow, in some societies it may entail us doing things that would be inappropriate ways of expressing love in another culture.

The important point to notice is that whatever wide rules we formulate or accept – whether it be respect for life or the rights of others, love for other human beings, or the 'Golden Rule' *Do to others as you would have them do to you*, or any other – they do have the force of rules. That means that we should accept that they represent obligations for us. They may not be precise and at times they may be difficult to apply, but they are still binding upon us.

ACTIVITY

In the light of what you have read, take a moment to think about how you make your moral decisions. Do you follow your intuitions? Do you have a set of rules that you follow? If so, what kind of rules are they? Do you use narrow rules that prescribe what you do or do not do in given situations? Perhaps in addition to some narrow rules or as an alternative, you have some clear principles that you then apply to whatever situation you are in. Do you use a combination of narrow and wide rules?

If you think that having rules is helpful or necessary, you may find

it helpful to write down what you think are the major rules
(whether narrow rules or wide rules) that

(a) guide your life, and

(b) should govern the lives of all Christians.

Are there any differences between your two lists?

Unit 3 **LOOKING AT THE RESULTS**

OBJECTIVES

When you have completed this unit you should be able to:

- *Appreciate why people differ in their views of what is of ultimate worth*

- *Appreciate some of the factors involved in deciding between alternative uses of resources*

- *Understand the difficulties in basing moral decisions on the outcomes of our actions*

- *Identify some of the limits of Christian enthusiasm.*

You may recall that Dana decided that in order to further the introduction of democracy into her country, she was prepared to lie about her knowledge of the presence of members of an underground movement. Her decision poses the question of the extent to which the *consequences* of our actions ought to affect our judgements. We certainly take note of possible outcomes to our behaviour and sometimes, as part of the way we teach children what is morally acceptable behaviour, we ask our children to think about the consequences of their actions. However, whilst we ask children, 'What if everyone did that?' it is not just a question for children. We also expect adults to bear this in mind when they think about their behaviour.

A couple facing marriage difficulties may decide to stay together 'for the good of the children'. In so doing they are usually looking at the possible outcomes of their decisions and deciding that to stay together will have a better outcome than separating. Our politicians justify their decisions by what they believe the long-term outcomes of their policies will be, and this kind of thinking lies behind their desire to avoid a 'boom or bust' economy.

As a general way of proceeding, this approach has a lot to commend it. It fits our general sense that the consequences of our actions are important to us and maybe to other people. Sometimes we think of them in terms of what will happen to us. Will my actions lead to a loss of money or status or face for me? Will telling a lie save me from painful consequences?

An awareness of the possible consequences of what we do may make us behave in ways that are selfish. Yet it may also make human beings behave in ways that we admire. A parent may go without new clothes or a holiday or food in order that a child might have a better life than would otherwise be possible. On Captain Scott's last expedition to the South Pole, Captain Oates walked out of the tent never to return, in the belief that his action would give his colleagues a better chance of reaching safety.

There is a long history of human beings acting in certain ways in the belief that in some way they will advance their cause. The Chinese communists endured the privations of the long march in order that their beliefs might survive and flourish and Christian martyrs give their lives for their faith.

Again and again the likely outcome of their actions causes men and women to decide to behave in certain ways rather than in others, and whilst we may think some of their actions are very worthy and others not so, we recognise that people like Dana act on the basis of what they believe to be the good outcome of what they do.

WHAT IS GOOD?

One of the reasons we may approve or disapprove of what they do, is whether we agree with their estimate of what counts as a good outcome. Some may think that adding to a large bank balance is a good outcome that justifies their actions. Others may claim that it does not justify any action. On the other hand the well-being and safety of others may justify sacrificing our own prospects and even our life.

The problem here is that we do not always agree on what the ultimate 'good' is. Most of us agree that health is a good thing and that things such as giving money to help the starving of Africa or supporting relief agencies, or promoting welfare services or opposing the closure of local hospitals, are justified because health is 'good'. But why is health to be valued and promoted? We could say that it is good because it gives us more choices in life. But why is it good to have more choices? We could answer in terms of self-fulfilment or personal growth, or simply as a way of promoting personal pleasure. But then why are these things good? So the search for an ultimate good continues, and because we disagree about it we may also disagree about the kind of behaviour we believe is justified and what we find unacceptable.

One of the most widely discussed and influential outcomes of our behaviour is the promotion of pleasure and the minimising of pain for the greatest number, and this influences the way in which politicians justify their policies and decisions, particularly near the time of a general election! There are some difficulties in such a view, the most obvious one being that of finding a way of *measuring* pleasure and pain. Try the exercise on the right.

TO THINK ABOUT...

Are there any ends that are so good that they justify the use of any means? Members of the Trumpton Independent Church are directing their energies to bringing men and women to faith in Jesus Christ, and they are doing it in the belief that this is one of their goals and purposes as disciples. For them it is a good end because there is nothing more important than the relationship between men and women, and Jesus. Are they justified in using any means to achieve it? If you think not, can you say what things are not justified? Why do you think such means are not justified, when the aim of helping people know God, is so good?

TO THINK ABOUT. . .

Think of two activities which will give you pleasure. Decide which of them gives most pleasure. Now ask yourself how you make that decision. Is it that one gives greater pleasure then the other? Or perhaps the pleasure you get from one lasts longer than that of the other. Is one a passing pleasure whilst you have pleasure from the other over a very long period? Is one tinged with pain whilst the other always gives you good feeling?

TO THINK ABOUT...

Suppose you are a government official and you have a limited amount of money which you can use in one of two ways. You can use it to give pleasure to many, many people by subsidising the opening of more Bingo halls, or you can give pleasure to fewer people by subsidising poetry readings. If you have to use the principle of maximising pleasure and minimising pain, how will you decide between them? Is it the number of people affected that guides your decision? Or is it the quality of the resulting pleasure that matters?

23

You may like to think about this problem of measuring pleasure in another way.

There is a further problem. Even if we agree that it is good to promote pleasure and minimise pain, do we decide to help a homeless family because, having looked at the situation, we decide that helping in this situation will promote more pleasure than pain for this particular family? Or do we decide to help them because we recognise a general principle which says that helping the homeless generally promotes pleasure and minimises pain.

LOVE AS A GOAL

The idea that the 'good' or 'end' is to be stated in terms of pleasure and pain has a long history, but there have been other suggestions as to what the end should be. One of the most important is that made by Joseph Fletcher in 1966 when he wrote in *Situation Ethics*, 'I have taken the procedure of doing ethics to be one of seeking the greatest amount of the 'good' possible for the greatest number of neighbours possible, and the standard of 'good' to be agape or loving concern for the neighbour – as judged by one's understanding of situations and human needs.'

Fletcher asks us to do two things. One is to see the 'good' as *love*; then he asks us to decide what is the loving thing to do in every situation. He does not accept that there are any moral rules which assume an intrinsic rightness of any action. The only rule to be followed is one of procedure rather than content, namely that we seek to show love by helping others and so do what is good, and seek to avoid whatever hurts others.

There is much in Fletcher's work that appeals to Christians. Jesus' teaching put love at the very heart of the way we treat each other, and Fletcher seems to reflect that. Further, he seeks the greatest amount of 'good' that is possible for the greatest number, and that too seems to be part of a Christian view of ethics. However, when we look carefully at some of the examples we can see some of the difficulties in seeing the moral question in terms of ends.

Fletcher gives a much quoted example of his argument in the story of Mrs Bergmeier, who at the end of World War II was held in a prison camp in the Ukraine. She learnt that after much searching, her husband had managed to gather together their scattered family. As Fletcher describes it, 'She more than anything else was needed to reknit them as a family in that dire situation of hunger, chaos and fear.' However, Mrs Bergmeier could only be released if she was in need of medical treatment only available outside the camp, or if she was pregnant. Finally she asked one of the guards to impregnate her, as a result of which she became pregnant and was sent back home to Berlin. When Dietrich was born he was loved by the family as being the cause of their reunion.

It would be easy to condemn Mrs Bergmeier, but then few of us can have been faced with her situation; she had to take a decision in the situation at that time, and not in the one she would have preferred.

You may have responded to Mrs Bergmeier's actions by saying that events could have turned out differently. She may have correctly guessed how her family would respond to news of her pregnancy but there may have been an element of doubt. Suppose her family had rejected Dietrich and her husband had been unable to accept that she deliberately became pregnant by another man? The difficulty is one that is often faced when we base our moral decision solely on the projected outcome of what we do. The crucial point here is that our actions do not always achieve the ends we have in mind.

> *TO THINK ABOUT…*
>
> *Before you read on, take a moment to ask yourself what you would have done in Mrs Bergmeier's situation. If you think she was morally wrong to become pregnant by the guard, ask yourself why. Remember that it could be claimed that she acted out of love for her family when she was needed, but do you think that is a sufficient justification for what she did?*
>
> *There is a further part of the story. On the day of Dietrich's christening Mr and Mrs Bergmeier went to their pastor to ask him whether they were right to feel so grateful for Dietrich and to think that he 'has done more for them than anyone.' How would you have answered them? If Mrs Bergmeier acted out of love, can her action be wrong, and if so, why?*

The first problem then in trying to decide whether an action is right or wrong by looking at the consequences, is that we do not always know what the consequences will be.

A second problem can be illustrated by thinking about the guard who fathered Dietrich. We might want to say that he was used by Mrs Bergmeier, and that it was wrong to ask him to commit adultery. It is easy to focus on the Bergmeier family and it may be true that the greatest 'good' was achieved for the greatest number, but was the means justified? Ought the guard to have been treated with more consideration, even though he may have been a willing participant? Did Mrs Bergmeier's moral obligation extend to him as well as to her family? Fletcher uses the incident to illustrate the way in which his view of love as a moral principle found expression in one situation, and if we accept his views we may say that in this case the ends do justify the means, because it was the most loving thing to do in that situation. Nevertheless, we may wish to question the morality of treating the guard as Mrs Bergmeier did.

The same problem exists in another of Fletcher's examples when he writes of President Truman's decision to drop the atomic bomb on two Japanese cities as 'a vast scale of agapeic calculus.' Over the years, it has been claimed that it was the loving thing to do because the lives saved probably exceeded the lives destroyed in the bombing. That may be true, but did the people who died deserve consideration as being more than mere statistics in a calculation of a likely death toll? Once again we can ask if the means were justified, no matter how worthy the end. It has to be said though, that few of us would like to have to take the decision that President Truman faced.

The strength of an attempt to build an ethic on what we see to be the likely outcome of our actions, is that it recognises the importance of taking account of the effects of our actions are likely to have. We can see those effects in terms of our own pleasures and desires, or we can evaluate them in the wider context of their effects on others as well as ourselves, and Fletcher is right in using love for our neighbours as his criterion for judging the moral worth of what we do.

This approach has the further virtue of recognising that no matter what approach we take, moral decision making is just that – decision making, not the application of rules that cover every eventuality, but a taking of decisions in the light of what we believe about what is right and wrong. That means that we may make the wrong decisions and we may not find that a very easy idea to accept.

So far we have thought about the strengths and weaknesses of looking at ethics from the point of view of rules and consequences, and we have been introduced to some of the complications that surround moral decision making, and cause different people to come to different conclusions about what is right and wrong. In the next unit we will begin to think about the way a Christian view of ethics may respond to complicated scenarios.

> **TO THINK ABOUT...**
>
> *Imagine you are a hospital consultant with very limited resources. You can use those resources to treat an elderly patient who has no relations but who is very active in helping those of his own generation who are housebound. Alternatively you can use them to treat a man who is the father of two young children. You have to make a choice. How would you do it?*

26

PART 2
A CHRISTIAN WAY

Unit 4 BACK TO BASICS

OBJECTIVES

When you have completed this unit you should be able to:

- *Survey the biblical basis of Christian living*

- *Understand why love and justice are important in Christian ethics*

- *Identify some of the positive principles behind biblical prohibitions*

- *Identify some of the motives behind the moral rules you and your church follow*

- *Understand the 'absolutes' of morality.*

In the previous units we have thought about the strengths and weaknesses of some of the ways in which we go about deciding whether an action is morally right or wrong. When we thought of Sophie's dilemma (whether or not to contemplate an abortion), we considered the possibility of making different kinds of *rules* which will enable us to know what we ought to do and will guide us in trying to shape society. Then when we thought about Dana's situation (whether or not to tell a lie), we looked at the possibility of using the likely *outcome* of our decisions as the measure of what is right and wrong.

If you are a Christian you may have found the previous units uncomfortable because they did not appear to be overtly Christian in their approach. Yet both approaches find their supporters among Christians, who claim to find them in scripture. The fact that Christians can support different views raises the question of whether Christian ethics is a matter of personal choice, or whether there is anything that, in their diversity, Christians ought to have in common.

It is worth remembering that the Bible was not written as an ethical textbook. It is part of the story of God, and that includes his relationship with men and women as they led their lives and attempted to relate to one another. In that context moral questions arose and decisions were taken, in some cases in the light of what God revealed to them, but always in the context of lives that were being lived out – and certainly not in the light of the attempts of ethicists to put some order to the variety of things that were done. In other words, biblical morality was primarily something that was *practised* rather than analysed and talked about.

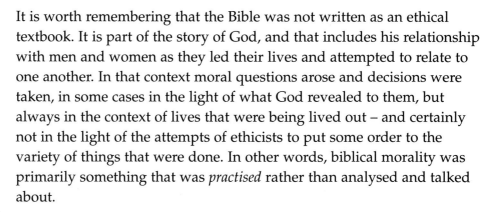

The same is true of Jesus' ethical teaching. Although Jesus embodied the moral standards and the kind of life that pleases his Father, he was not primarily a teacher of ethics. He was the bearer of the good news of the love of God, who showed that love in his life and death. His ethical teaching is essentially his response to the day to day events of life and to the ways in which the people around him reacted to them. As such it leaves us without a codified system of ethics which answers all the detailed questions we want to ask, and it certainly does not directly tell us what approach we should use in forming a Christian ethic. We are left with a number of examples of Jesus 'doing' ethics by dealing with ethical questions in the context of the harsh realities of life. The result is that we do not have a systematic or theoretical ethic from Jesus. It was practical and fashioned by the needs of men and women in concrete situations, and that means that we have to abstract the basis of his method of doing ethics from the way in which he approached people's concerns and related to them.

Although this background may not make it easy to decide what is a Christian approach to ethics, when we look at the ethical teaching that is in the Bible there are some things which we can abstract from its pages, that will give us the basis of a Christian approach.

WHY BE GOOD?

The first thing we can note is that we are invited to live according to God's way, because that is the right response to what God has done. We can see it in a number of places. Before the first of the Ten Commandments in Exodus 20, God set the context in which they were given. '"I am the Lord your God, who brought you out of the land of Egypt, out of the house of slavery"' (Exodus 20:2). It was because of what God had done that his people were to live according to his ways.

Paul made the same appeal when he wrote to the Romans, 'Therefore, brothers, because God has been so merciful to us, I urge you to offer yourselves a living sacrifice, holy and acceptable to him; for this is the true way of worshipping him' (Romans 12:1). And then the apostle goes on to talk of the way in which Christians should relate to one another. Once again, our behaviour should be an appropriate response to what God has done for us.

We can express this in another way. When God freed the children of Israel from slavery in Egypt he made a covenant with them. It was later summed up, '"They will be my people and I will be their God"' (Jeremiah 24:7). It speaks of a relationship with God. When someone gets married and enters into a new relationship with their partner, there are certain expectations about the kind of responses that will express the new commitment. Similarly when we have a relationship with God he invites us to respond to him in the way we lead our lives. John put it this way, 'Dear friends, if God loved us in this way we also ought to love one another' (1 John 4:11). Jesus too made the same point when he said, '"If you love me you will keep my commandments"' (John 14:15). Paul echoes it in Romans 6 when he speaks of the consequences of being baptised into Jesus Christ, 'We were therefore buried with him through baptism into death in order that, just as Christ was raised from the dead through the glory of the Father, we too may live a new life' (Romans 6:4). The first question then in Christian ethics is not 'what ought we to do?', but rather 'what has God done for us?'

Any biblical approach needs to include the way in which the motivation for living a life that is pleasing to God arises from what God has done for us and from the relationship we have with God, even though there are different ways of expressing this relationship. Some Christians act as though they are under a court order from God that decrees what they can and cannot do. On this account, morality becomes a duty which we have to do in obedience to God. Other Christians see it as a love affair between God and human beings.

> *TO THINK ABOUT...*
>
> *Before you read further, pause and ask yourself what it is that makes you want to live in a way that is right for a Christian. Try to be honest with yourself.*

A BASIS FOR ETHICS

The second thing to notice is that the relationship we have with the creator God means that our behaviour ought to be rooted in the nature of God. He reaches out to us in love and grace, enters into a relationship

29

with us and then invites us to repeat that same act with others. The whole enterprise is not simply a pragmatic convenience which enables us to live in harmony with one another. It stems from the nature of God which is essentially one of love, and what God required of people in scripture is nothing more nor less than a reflection of what he, himself, is.

We share in God's enterprise which comes from his nature of love, and which reflects who he is. The first commandment that '"You shall have no other gods before me"', is at the heart of Christian morality. It is a call, not simply to obey God because he is the Lord, but to be what God is in his own moral nature. This is reflected in the charge, '"You shall be holy, for I the Lord your God am holy"' (Leviticus 19:2).

The psalmist wrote, 'All the ways of the Lord are loving and faithful' (Psalm 25:10). They are so because that is his nature, and to think that his moral standards involve anything that is unloving or unfaithful is to imply that he contradicts himself. When the Bible calls us to a life of faithfulness and goodness and integrity, to respect life and property and to love one another, it is a call to act in accordance with the character of God himself and to live lives that reflect his character. This is in harmony with Paul's exhortation, 'Therefore be imitators of God, as beloved children; and walk in love, just as Christ also loved you, and gave himself up for us' (Ephesians 5:1).

One of the implications of this is that what he asks of us is as permanent as God himself. Whatever his moral standards are, and we have yet to discuss what they may be, at one level they must be such that they do not change with different cultures or at different times or in different situations. The reason is that the character of God does not change and his moral expectations of those who respond to him are so integral to his character, that they do not change either.

MORALITY: OUR RESPONSE TO GOD'S PRIOR ACTION

Having recognised that our morality should be a response to what God has done, and that it should reflect his nature, we can move on to look more closely at what a Christian approach might be.

For some of us, our first ideas about Christian ethics centred on the Ten Commandments with its list of things we ought not to do. *'Thou shalt not...'* is a view of the Christian life that sees it as a set of narrow restrictive laws which lay down those things that are inappropriate for Christians to do, and this is taken to be the Christian ethic.

However, before we settle for that view, there are two things to notice about the Commandments.

First, the Ten Commandments are very limited in scope. They refer to important aspects of life, but nevertheless they are few in number. It is true that there are other commandments in the Bible that we need to take note of as well, but even when we take those into account there is a distinct shortage of specific rules that will deal with all the complexities of life. If God meant us to base our morality solely on narrow, specific rules, then we can at least ask if what we have is sufficient.

Second, the specific rules that we have are negative expressions of positive principles and are a summary of standards that had been already recognised and observed. The moral law was in the hearts of people before it was put on the stone tablets. For example, when Joseph accused his brothers of stealing his silver cup, they recognised the moral significance of his charge (Genesis 44:4–7). The moral dimension of murder is recognised in the story of Cain and Abel, '"Where is your brother Abel?"' (Genesis 4:9). Joseph was invited to commit adultery with Potiphar's wife, and he described it as 'this great evil' (Genesis 39:9).

Negative prohibitions are only part of the moral story and we recognise that in the way we teach our children. When they are young we tell them what not to do – "do not touch that" – "do not say *that* to your friend" – "you must not go around hitting other children", and so on. That is how young children learn that there are some ways of behaving that are morally wrong. It is a concrete way of learning that does not require any ability to deal with abstract ideas, and for that reason it is available to even the very young. But as well as teaching them those things that are forbidden, there comes a time when we also help them to learn the positive principles that underlie them. So we teach them that animals must be cared for, promises should be kept, and we ought to take care of other people's belongings. These are the positive principles which are often better taught and reinforced by negative prohibitions.

"DON'T DO THAT DEAR"

Many of the commandments that appear in various parts of the Bible are the negative implications of positive principles, and they are some of the details of how the basic principles of God's way of life are worked out. Moreover they are in a form that is easily remembered.

If we relate our discussion so far to chapter 2, then the narrow rules that are so often taken to characterise Christian ethics are expressions of much wider rules which act as principles which we can use to guide and direct our lives. Moreover, it is *these principles* which are basic to Christian living, and not the narrow rules.

This view finds some support from the way in which Jesus handled what was seen as the law. When a teacher of the law asked him which is the chief commandment of the law, Jesus replied, '"You must love the Lord your God with all your heart, with all your soul, and with all your mind. This is the chief and first commandment. The second is like it: you must love your neighbour as yourself"' (Matthew 22:36–40). That is familiar to us. What follows tells us something more about Jesus' thinking: '"On these two commandments the whole Law and Prophets depend."' The twofold command to love God and our neighbours is the peg on which all the other commands and exhortations and invitations hang. To obey and follow them is to express love. This is what we should expect, for love is at the heart of who God is, and is the right response to the God who loves us and the whole of his creation.

It means that at the heart of moral life is love. It is all about the expression of love, so that our moral responsibility to God and to those around us can be summed up as being an obligation to love, and to do it wholeheartedly, with heart and soul and mind.

ACTIVITY

Read the following passages which give us some of the things that should characterise our lives when we follow Jesus Christ. If you are able to do this with another person, discuss together what it is about the qualities that are mentioned that makes them expressions of love. If you are working on your own, write down your answers.

> *Romans 12:9–18*
> *Ephesians 4:28–29*

Now do the same with the following passage, but this time say why the behaviour that is described is unloving and does not reflect the nature of God.

> *Galatians 5:19–21*

To summarise so far then – it is biblical teaching that love is the overriding principle that is to govern our moral life, so that the way Christians behave towards God and other people is to be an expression of love. This is to say that Christian ethics is not a series of narrow rules which at times seems to be about the things we should not do. It rests on the principle that love should inform and determine our behaviour.

JUSTICE: LOVE IN ACTION

So far we have been trying to grapple with statements in the Bible which give the impression that the moral implication of being a Christian is that we have to live by a number of specific commands, and we have seen that Jesus saw the whole matter as living a life based on love. But we have to acknowledge that as a principle, love is very general. In Unit 3 we saw that Joseph Fletcher tried to make it more specific, by referring to the greatest amount of love possible for the greatest number of neighbours possible. The Bible has another way that helps make it more specific, and that is to place it alongside the need for justice.

In the Bible, justice is a major concern of God's. It is not a theoretical commitment to justice as 'a good thing'. God *does* justice. 'The Lord works righteousness and justice for all the oppressed' (Psalm 103:6). As you read the Old Testament you will see that it is part of God's character of love that he wants to see that the weak and vulnerable receive justice.

Justice is separate from love, yet they need each other. One of the important tasks of both of them is to see that our humanity is respected and that we have the opportunity to become and function more fully as human beings. To this end, justice may act as a brake on some of the excesses of love, preserving our humanity. Yet love does the same thing when the interests of justice treat us as objects to be judged. The two are separate then, but they are complementary.

So God's invitation to us to respond to what he has done, and to reflect his own character, means that we live lives that are based on the basic principles of love and justice.

Our discussion in this unit has led us to see that

- If we are to handle some of the moral issues that arise in our own times, the Bible is of little help if it only contains commands and injunctions that apply to specific situations. Moral dilemmas such as whether eggs from dead women ought to be used in the treatment of infertility were not part of the biblical world. On pragmatic grounds then, if we are to use the Bible in making moral decisions, we need principles which transcend the centuries and which we can apply to the moral life of our own times.

- The need for principles is not simply a pragmatic matter. We have seen that love and justice are principles which we can use in any culture or at any time, and that they are at the root of a biblical approach to ethics.

- God's invitation to us is not to obey a set of rules out of a sense of duty, but to respond to what he has done and continues to do for us. Moreover it is an invitation to live in harmony with his character, and to reflect the love and sense of justice that underlies his dealings with us.

Although we have established that these principles are at the heart of a Christian way of life, we need to look more closely at them in order to consider how we might understand them, and this is what the next three units are about.

Unit 5 LOVE ONE ANOTHER

OBJECTIVES

When you have completed this unit you should be able to:

- *Appreciate why it is difficult to live by the principle of love*

- *Understand the view you take of the place of rules in living a life of love*

- *Survey different ways in which rules may relate to love*

- *Identify how far you think love should involve rules.*

Love is not only the most basic principle of Christian ethics, it is also one of the most difficult to pin down and give some substance to. There is a romantic sense of love which gives us strange indescribable sensations, but there is another sense in which we behave towards each other in ways that express the care and concern and commitment that we call 'love'. Before we go further, try the following exercise to explore what kind of things you think are loving actions.

ACTIVITY
Think of someone whom you love and who you think loves you - maybe a parent or a partner or a child or a friend. Spend a few minutes writing down the kind of action that show your love for that person, and what they do which tells you that they love you.

When we were children we learnt something of the meaning of love as we saw and experienced various things that we were told were signs of love. Perhaps it was a mother's request for a kiss which she said would be a sign that her child loved her. Maybe we learnt the word in the context of seeing two people with their arms about each other. Maybe we saw two people parting and shedding tears. Or maybe in learning about the intimacy of sexual intercourse we learnt that the word 'love' was applicable there too. As children we probably had our own criteria for love, and when one of our classmates fulfilled them we said, 'you love her' – to everyone's embarrassment!

As we grow older we realise that these early ideas need refining. We may become quite skilful at spotting people whom we think are in love, by noticing a glance or a smile, but we find that at times we are mistaken. We come to realise, sometimes painfully, that what we assume are expressions of love are not always so. We learn that the signs of love can be counterfeited, and slowly we come to accept that love means different things to different people, and that at times it shows in strange ways. This can all create problems for us when we want to say what love means, not least when, as Christians, we want to love our neighbours. How then, do we decide what is the loving way to behave?

DECIDING HOW TO BEHAVE

One of the ways we use is to look at our common experience of those times when we have known love to be present, and to make some further general principles which we believe represent acts of love. This may lead us to say that in our experience, keeping promises are loving actions. They show a respect for the people we deal with and actually help them to make the decisions and choices they think best. Our experience may tell us that a damaged environment restricts what people can do with their lives and makes it hard for some of them to be their true selves, because the stress of struggling with evils like pollution and drought distorts their lives. So we may decide that it is a loving thing to fight to protect the environment. To claim, as some do, that adversity helps to form character may be true, but that does not take away our responsibility to give people the best conditions possible in which to live and grow and be truly human, and that is a loving thing to do.

Obviously if there are general principles, such as 'tell the truth' or 'protect the environment', that we can agree reflect loving actions, they will help to give some structure to what we should do. However, when we were thinking about the place of rules in ethics (Unit 2), we thought about the way in which rules could be rigidly applied or used as guiding principles which could be set aside when necessary. The same alternative is present when we try to make principles that reflect loving ways of treating people and creation. Such principles themselves can be held rigidly or used as guides.

We could decide that to love is to *always* keep promises and *never* allow the environment to become unusable. If we make our principles so rigid they become like acts of Parliament rather than laws of nature, but it is a way of fixing safeguards that ensure that we always fulfil our obligation to show love.

The alternative is to decide that in the overwhelming number of cases, love is expressed by such things as keeping promises and protecting the environment, but that we do not want to close the door on the possibility that there may be cases where, for example, it would be more loving to break a promise or deliberately destroy an area of great beauty. It is not to say that we would do such things whenever the urge took us, but that we think there may be times when love dictates what are unusual actions.

ADHERING TO THE RULES

Apart from the obvious fact that having and applying these general principles or rules that express love helps us to be clear about what we believe, and avoids any misunderstanding about what the Christian faith stands for, there are other arguments that have been advanced in favour of this approach.

One is that some sort of rules are an essential part of love. Love does not operate in a vacuum, but through rules. We can point to the Ten Commandments and say that they are an expression of love, so that the loving thing to do is to insist that the commandments be kept. It may not always be easy, but nevertheless that is what has to be done, because in the end that is to people's benefit.

"AN EXPRESSION OF LOVE"

TO THINK ABOUT...

Bert was temporarily short of cash and borrowed £500 from a close friend on the understanding that he would repay the loan by the 18th of the month. Imagine his horror when he heard that his friend planned to use the repaid loan to take advantage of a special offer to invest in a company publishing pornography. The offer closed on the 20th. Bert was extremely disturbed by this as he was totally against such publications, yet he prided himself on keeping his promises. What do you think is the loving thing for Bert to do? Repay on time, knowing what the money will be used for, or delay and in so doing break his promise?

Does your answer imply that in this case you believe that love requires that Bert's moral principle should not be set aside, or that there are exceptions to the principle?

Another argument in favour of a tight set of rules expressing love, is that love must act through rules because this is the way the world is constituted and love can only find its full expression through rules which God has laid down.

You may want to support another idea, namely that which says that we are all part of a created order of things which requires that certain rules be followed if we are to 'follow the maker's instructions' and live in harmony with our own created nature as humans, and with the natural world. An example would be the claim that having one marriage partner is the 'natural' arrangement which matches the created order. The claim could then go on to say that this is shown in the jealousy which can arise in households in which there is more than one wife.

TO THINK ABOUT...

Check your reactions to these ideas as you think about the following situation that a couple faced. See how you respond.

A marriage has 'died'. There are no third persons involved, but both partners recognise that their relationship is now empty of any real meaning and they no longer take comfort from or find support in the other person. They realise it has reached a point where they cannot hope to revive what they once had.

Do you think it is a loving thing to require the couple to continue to live in the same house, when they can no longer relate to one another? What does your answer tell you about your view of love? Does it show that your position is one of those which require rules for the application of love?

The couple go to their pastor who insists that for them to split would be wrong because there are rules which the Christian church should follow and standards it should defend. For them to part would be a bad witness.

If you were the pastor, what do you think would be the best justification of your view, whilst at the same time claiming that love is at the heart of your gospel?

The pastor's view certainly upholds the idea of the sanctity of marriage and it gives a clear message that his church is against what they take to be an abuse of a sacred alliance. The clear message is that marriage is a good thing and that we ought to do all we can to support that fact. There is an implication in this though, namely that the state of marriage is of greater significance than individual couples within it. You may agree with this, or you may feel that love requires more than the observance of rules.

The problem with rule-governed love is that whilst we may automatically apply moral rules which we believe express love, to many people the very idea of love transcends rules. For example, the generation that went to Woodstock in 1969 were seeking love and peace that were unfettered by rules. They confronted their world with love as it was perceived in their situation at their time. There is something attractive about the idea that all we need is love, so that we treat one another as individuals, respecting each other's freedom to be ourselves, and caring for one another. It is the attraction of a life which is unfettered by hidebound, unthinking conventions and what may be irrational prejudices.

Yet despite the attraction, such a view is open to abuse. In the name of love a person can satisfy their own desires, and as the criteria for love are so ill-defined, it may be hard to identify whether actions are those of love or not. Even where there is a desire to love, such a view has an assumption that we have a built-in moral compass that in the name of love will draw us to what is morally right. It is not obviously so.

TO THINK ABOUT…

Tom and Mary are deeply committed to one another in love. They share the deepest things in their lives and both seek to give themselves to the other. Tom and Mary are not yet married, though they are engaged and hope that one day soon they will be husband and wife. They admit to a friend that they feel that their love and sense of oneness finds its ultimate expression in a sexual relationship.

(a) In the light of this story, do you think there may be situations like that of Tom and Mary, where what appears to be love transcends the usual norms of human behaviour?

(b) If you answer YES, do you want to draw a line somewhere? Under what circumstances would their case be acceptable to you and in what circumstances would it be unacceptable?

(c) If you answer NO, what view are you taking about the way we decide on moral behaviour that is in the name of love, and reflects our view of love?

Yet even with the possibility of abuse that this view contains, we have to accept that sometimes people do claim to act out of a sense of love, even though the actual behaviour may not meet our normal expectations of Christian behaviour.

Although it is dangerous to be selective in using scripture, check what you think about love and rules, by reading the following passage from The Translator's New Testament.

We have to accept that whilst it is convenient and helpful for us to decide on rules that reflect love, some Christians find that they restrict what they take to be love. Whatever view we take, we have seen that if we are to reflect the nature of God, we need to think of love in the context of what is the just thing to do. Like love, what constitutes justice is not obviously clear, and so in the next unit we will turn our attention to trying to understand what it might be.

Unit 6 DO JUSTICE

OBJECTIVES

When you have completed this unit you should be able to:

- *Survey biblical views of justice*
- *Understand the principles on which we decide if actions are just or unjust*
- *Apply the principle of justice to some of the issues in your church or community*
- *Examine some claims for positive discrimination.*

There is a long-standing tradition that God's justice is shown as he seeks retribution from those who violate his law, even though Jesus refuted such an idea. Perhaps it is more correct to say that in the Bible, God's concern for justice centres far more on those for whom there is no justice. It is in this sense that Isaiah writes, "'I, the Lord, love justice; I hate robbery and iniquity'" (Isaiah 61:8).

It could be claimed that justice is simply an aspect of love in that it is an act of love to see those who are worth loving as being worth defending from oppression and exploitation, and seeing that they receive a fair chance. However we describe the relationship between love and justice, if human worth is to be truly recognised, we need both of them. They complement one another and add to each the checks and balances that both need if they are not to be abused.

The fact is that we can be thoroughly just in what we do, but not show much love in the process. It is one of the dangers of being an official and having authority, that in the way we deal with people we lose the element of love that recognises their humanity.

This can be seen in all kinds of ways in our daily lives, but Mrs Johnson illustrates the point. She was a receptionist in the accident department of the local hospital, and everyone agreed that she was very efficient. She knew exactly what needed to be done and did it. She saw to it that patients were seen in order and that their paperwork was correct and complete. To the medical staff she was a treasure. Mrs Johnson seemed to be aware of those who would try to jump the queue with the excuse that they had to be somewhere else in ten minutes. The patients were all kept in order and it was a matter of pride for Mrs Johnson that everyone was seen in the order in which they came. Unfortunately her system seemed to be so important that at times she had little sympathy for patients. She had a job to do and patients had to do their part so that she could do it.

It could be said, and in Mrs Johnson's case it was said, that she was very fair and efficient but did not show much love for the patients.

One of her colleagues, Mrs James, would fuss around the elderly patients and if necessary, rather than requiring them to wait at her desk,

TO THINK ABOUT…

Mrs Johnson and Mrs James treated the patients in different ways. Do you think either of them acted justly? If so, which one?

she would tell them to sit down and she would go to them to get the details she needed. She had been known to make sure that distressed patients, particularly frightened children, were seen as soon as a doctor was free, rather than having to wait their turn. At those times Mrs Johnson always took her to task and said that she was being unfair to the rest of the patients, yet it was generally agreed that Mrs James was loving and caring in the way she did the job.

It is not only that we can deny a person's humanity in the name of justice – there are also times when it can be done in the name of love. There are some parents who do this with their children. It can take many forms. Some will not let their children grow up and become independent of them. Others indulge their children so much that they do not learn that being human means we respect the needs of others. In the name of love, others are over-protective. Love can be sentimentalised to the point where the good of the person who is loved is actually limited, to the detriment of their humanity.

Over the years we have learned to talk of justice in terms that reflect our experiences. Events happen and we learn that it is appropriate to talk of justice or, perhaps more often, injustice. We will limit our discussion to two contexts in which we talk of justice, both of which are relevant to helping us form our ideas about morality.

RESPONSIBILITY

The first has already been implied, namely that sometimes we speak of justice when we want to affirm our right to be treated as fully responsible human beings. Experienced teachers sometimes think they have spotted trouble-makers in a new class, before they have done anything wrong. They notice the way the other children look at them and seem to be waiting for something to happen. Or the teacher notices the look on the faces of some children, and recognises potential trouble. It would be possible to inflict some kind of unpleasantness on such a child *before* there were any misdemeanours, and that may act as a deterrent, but we would probably say that was unjust. The reason is that it does not allow the child to be responsible for what happens. If he does do something wrong we would accept that he is responsible and do something about it. But most of us would probably think it is right to let the child himself take the responsibility of deciding to misbehave or not, and with it, take the consequences. We will return to this later when we look in more detail at issues surrounding punishment. We generally accept then, that it is just to let human beings take responsibility for what they do, unless we have grounds for thinking they cannot take it, in which case we help them.

Before we go on to think about a second idea of justice, try to answer the following question.

ACTIVITY

In your opinion, which, if any, of the following best describes what justice is?

(a) *Making sure that everyone has the role in society for which they are best suited.*

(b) *Promoting a society which defends the rights of all and gives everyone an equal chance in life.*

(c) *A society is just when there is the greatest happiness that is possible.*

If you are dissatisfied with these descriptions, try to write down your own description.

At different times each of the above has been advocated by serious thinkers, so if you agree with any of them, you are in good company.

Now let us turn to the second idea of justice.

THE BIBLICAL VIEW OF JUSTICE

The Bible has a lot to say about justice, though as we might expect, it is not in the form of abstract definitions. God is a lover of justice, and it is his will that justice be done. Typical of statements about God and justice, is 'I know that the Lord will maintain the cause of the afflicted, and justice for the poor' (Psalm 140:12). God promised to 'raise up for David a righteous Branch; he will reign as king and act wisely and do justice and righteousness in the land' (Jeremiah 23:5). Again and again there are references to God's concern for justice, particularly in the books of the prophets Isaiah, Micah and Amos. They wrote of God being more concerned about the injustice that was being shown the poor and vulnerable in society, than for the way in which religious ceremonies and feasts were kept and the careful way in which the right offerings were made. 'Let justice roll down like waters, and righteousness like an ever-flowing stream' (Amos 5:21–24) sums up much of the social concern shown in the prophets. The God of the prophets is a practical God who cares about what happens to people, particularly when they are treated unjustly.

In the Old Testament, justice was concerned with meeting the needs of the deprived – the poor, the afflicted, the vulnerable and the oppressed members of society. It was not simply that there was a sympathetic compassion for them, but rather, it was a call for the protection of those who in some way were unable to obtain what was rightly theirs in a society where people were meant to be independent. It was a concern for those who did not get a fair share of the resources that society has. So far so good, but we still want to know what constitutes 'justice'. What is the content of this principle? How does it work?

To give us a situation on which to reflect, let us take the case of a black girl called Stella, who works in an office. She is good at her job, personable and she is good in her relations with her colleagues and the general public whom she has to meet. But over a period of time it becomes clear to her and some of her colleagues that people who joined the firm after her, and in some cases know less about the job than she does, are being given more responsibility, whilst Stella's chances of promotion appear to be growing less. One of her friends asks her why she thinks this is, and she replies that it was probably all to do with the colour of her face. Her friend's response is to ask what that has to do with it.

The point he sensed was that the colour of Stella's skin was irrelevant when it came to promotion, and because of that, Stella was the victim of an injustice.

In the same way we would think it unjust if people with painted finger nails were always served first in restaurants. What have painted finger nails to do with being served? Unless there is something further that we do not know about the story, we say, *nothing*.

In these cases we are using a principle that says that as a matter of justice, we should treat people in the same way unless there are good, relevant reasons why we should make distinctions between them. For example, most of us recognise that there is some justice in a boy who needs a wheel chair being taken to the front of the crowd at a football match, so that he can have a view that is uninterrupted by people jumping up and down in front of him. The fact that he is confined to a wheel chair is a relevant reason for him to be treated in this way.

On the other hand, if we decide it is fair that one boy in a wheel chair goes to the front of the crowd, it is also fair that other people in wheel chairs go to the front. In so far that they are all in wheel chairs and assuming there are no other relevant differences between them, they should receive the same consideration.

Our principle in short is: where there are relevant differences people should be treated differently, but where there are no relevant differences they should be treated in the same way.

" THE CHURCH LEADERSHIP TEAM "

This view of justice is one we can recognise in the Old Testament prophets. In their times there was a lot of injustice. In Amos 2 and 5 for example, the prophet speaks of some of the social ills of his time. The poor man was abused by landsharks who could take advantage of his powerlessness by making loans that could not be repaid, and then taking the land as payment for the debt. In some cases men even sold themselves into slavery in order to meet their obligations. The law was meant to protect the disadvantaged, but had been so distorted in favour of the powerful that the poor could be robbed of what they had. In chapter 8 the prophet speaks of the dishonest scales that robbed the poor. The prophets' task was to recall people to God's original intentions, so in the context of such a catalogue of abuse, the prophet calls for justice.

A major part of the book of Amos is about the question, Why should the poor be taken advantage of? They were the despised of the land, but was that a relevant ground for driving them into further poverty? Is poverty an adequate reason why some should be denied a fair hearing in the courts? Is it a good ground for using scales which have been doctored to take advantage of the poor? The biblical view is that the poor should be protected in order that their humanity is respected.

At the heart of the prophet's concern is the charge that this principle of justice has not been applied, and because of it he has to say, 'Hate evil, love good, and establish justice in the gate' (Amos 5:15).

In his book *The Theory of Justice*, John Rawls suggested that one way of understanding what a just society would look like is to imagine that we had the opportunity to restructure society. If none of those charged with the job knew where they would fit into the new society, the outcome would be one in which those at the bottom of society would be protected, and have a protected minimum standard of life. It is the same principle that Jesus gave his disciples, '"Treat men just as you want them to treat you"' (Luke 6:31).

ACTIVITY

Using John Rawls' idea, talk to some of your friends and see what you think are the necessities that are required for a minimum standard of acceptable life in your town or village or church.

The concept of justice is a basic principle then, which is fundamental to moral life. Along with love, it provides the basis of our Christian ethics by giving expression to the worth of human beings. It is the expression of the very nature of the God who loves the weak and defenceless.

We have spent some time establishing the basis of a view of Christian ethics, because it is important to our understanding of what ethics is all about. We have thought about the importance of love and justice, and seen something of what we might mean by them. Their significance is enormous, because these are the moral absolutes we so often seek. They are unchanging and unchangeable, simply because they are the basic expressions of who God is, and to respond to him means behaving in love and with justice. There are no options here. These are the obligations laid upon those who claim to follow Christ, and whatever differences Christians might have on moral issues, they should arise from the different ways in which it is possible to express love and justice.

As a way of beginning to link love and justice with our daily lives, the next unit will introduce the important idea of being human.

Unit 7 FULL STATURE

OBJECTIVES

When you have completed this unit you should be able to:

- *Identify some of the times when you have or have not been respected as a human being*
- *Appreciate the intrinsic worth of human beings*
- *Understand the ways in which society sometimes diminishes human worth*
- *Understand the structure of moral decision making.*

To think about morality is to think about people. If we pause and think about those parts of life that we put under the heading of 'moral', we see that they are about the way we behave and think, the attitudes we have, and the relationships we form with each other and with the world around us. We may talk as though there is a morality in the animal kingdom, but that is about the way we human beings treat animals, and about our relationship with them, not their relationship with us or with each other. Indeed, by human standards, animals themselves do appalling things to each other, but we do not talk of them behaving immorally. So morality is about humans. It is a 'person' ethic.

We have seen that a Christian view of ethics starts from the nature of God, and it has been suggested that it finds its basic expression in love and justice, which are expressions of who and what God is. In this unit, we think about the way in which love and justice both make assumptions about the nature of human beings.

Check out this statement in doing the following.

> **ACTIVITY**
> *Look at the story of the rich young man in Mark 10:17–22. In v. 21 it says that Jesus was filled with love for him. What do you think caused that love?*

UNDERSTANDING OUR WORTH

There is a tradition that says that human beings are thoroughly evil, so much so that there is no good in them at all. The element of truth in this is that we are unable to meet God's standards. It can be misleading though if it is meant to imply that we are thereby of no worth in God's eyes. John says that *(God) loved us and sent his Son as the means of taking away our sins*. Clearly, God has a tremendously high view of us. No matter how bad we may be or how deep rooted that might be, there is something about us human beings that God loves, to the point of sending his only Son to die as an outcast. This is the evidence that shows how much we mean to God. One of the features of the gospel is that God's love recognises the depths to which we can sink, yet even so, God still loves us – even the unlovely who would reject his love. God's love, then, is based on a very high view of our worth.

Some Christians believe that the worth of human beings is to be seen in the way God works out his plan of salvation. However, the same worth is also to be found in the biblical view of creation. The creation stories are not there to provide an intellectual account of how things began. They tell us that right from the beginning, human beings were to be of such worth in God's view that he made them in his own image. How much more special can we be than that? It means we were made to be like God in some way. It is no wonder that God loves not just those who want to please him, but the whole of created humanity – warts and all!

Similarly, the way in which the prophets speak of God's concern that people be treated fairly, carries the implication that people matter. It is no accident that those who are denied justice sometimes feel demeaned as persons, because they feel they do not have any worth or a place in society. Yet the teaching of the creation stories is that people have been so formed that they bear the imprint of God himself. The result is that even though they may be treated badly, they are of such value that their well-being and their dignity ought to be respected. That means that there is something about us, in our very humanity, that means that each of us has an obligation to treat others fairly.

So a fundamental assumption of Christian ethics, which underlies its principles of love and justice, is that human beings are *valuable to God*, and because of that, our humanity ought to be respected and treated with love and justice.

UNDERSTANDING OUR HUMANITY

As we have seen, love and justice are basic to Christian ethics, but they are abstract and need to be applied and given substance. One way of beginning to flesh them out, is to begin to identify some of the features that constitute the humanity that they assume.

For example, one of the features of being human is that we are damaged. In various ways and for various reasons we carry the marks of the past. As we understand more of the effects of our upbringing and experiences, so we recognise more of the fears and defence mechanisms, hang-ups and false faces we have developed to help us cope with life. It is because we are 'damaged goods' that some of us behave the way we do. For example, because of parental drive and expectations in our youth, we may not be able to handle failure in our lives. To that extent our past affects who we are today.

This element of damage to our humanity can be quite frightening and bewildering in some people's lives. Some people become outrageously irrational. Some become defensive, whilst others see the world as a place marked by changes, each of which is a threat to the status quo with which we feel comfortable. Others commit acts that to the rest of us may appear to be morally wrong, yet that raises the question we met in Unit 1 about John exceeding the speed limit. Can we always be held responsible for the things we do that do not express love? There is no question about the need to love and act justly, but there are times when we have to accept our very limited ability to do that adequately, not least because to learn to love others we need to be loved ourselves, and some people experience little love.

In his book *New Directions in Moral Theology*, Kevin Kelly quotes a story from Josef Fuchs. It is a Hassidic legend: 'Before his death Rabbi Sussja said, "In the world to come, I will not be asked, 'Why are you not Moses?' I will be asked, 'Why were you not Sussja?'"' The truth the legend contains is that being a human person means accepting responsibility, not only for *what we do*, but also for *who we are*. That in

turn means letting each other have the freedom in which to exercise that responsibility. Unfortunately many lives are bound by paternalistic individuals and groups who want to take control of us and shape us to be the kind of person they want us to be, and to ensure that we live in ways they decree.

RESPECTING OUR PERSONHOOD

TO THINK ABOUT...

In the light of the need to let each other take responsibility for our own lives, do you think women should be able to take their own decisions as to what to do when faced with an unwanted pregnancy? Or should abortion be legally controlled? Which is the most just and loving of these two options?

In making this choice we are only considering one of the factors involved in the abortion debate.

One of the loving things we can do for each other is to let one another have the space to take control of our own lives and to respect our personhood. One of the great acts of parental love is letting children have the space in which to form their own lives and discover who they are. We may not always like the results and it may be a very painful experience, but at times love is painful.

Respecting the humanity of others is one thing. Respecting our own humanity is another, particularly for busy people who have a strong desire to serve others. There is a love which centres on ourselves, often to the detriment of others. But there is also a healthy self-love which recognises that we need to take care of ourselves and to become what we were meant to be. It is a misunderstanding to think that self-love automatically means that others will be ignored or hurt. Loving ourselves, and hence being what we are meant to be, has a social dimension and carries with it the responsibility for helping them to grow as persons. In practice, it is often the people who have a healthy regard for their own humanity, and who love themselves as they are, who are best able to help others.

When Jesus spoke of us loving our neighbours as ourselves, it implied that we *do* love ourselves and that such love is the measure of our love for others.

Self-love can mean legitimately saying 'no' to some of the demands people make on us, at times even the demands of our immediate family. It can mean making our own choices of life style. It means claiming who we are as a person, made in the image of God and of immeasurable value, and then living on that basis. In other words, it means claiming our own and others' humanity from all that would diminish and degrade it. To do this is to practice love and justice, for they have at their heart the acknowledgement of the valued humanity of ourselves and our fellow human beings, and a desire to promote that humanity in all its fullness.

Just a little thought about what it means to be human, gives us some directions as to what love and justice mean. To show love to some people may mean protecting them from those things that would diminish their quality of life as human beings, whilst justice can mean ensuring that they get that quality to the fullest extent.

> ### *ACTIVITY*
> *Jane is a single mother living with her child in one room. List some of the things that you and your church may need to do if you respect her human dignity, and want to act in a loving and just way towards her.*

Our damaged humanity has two consequences for the way in which we exercise love and justice:

- In whatever form this damaged self shows itself in others, it never excuses us from showing them love and acting justly towards them.

- As we decide what are the loving things to do and think, we need to bear in mind that we too are damaged, and that can affect the way and the extent to which we love others. We love and act justly with all the limitations and defence mechanisms, fears and prejudices, that are a part of who we are. Even so, they do not limit our obligation to show love and justice to the best of our ability, for they reflect our value of our common humanity.

TAKING STOCK

Before we think further about the way in which love and justice may be used to guide our moral thinking, it will be helpful to pause and take stock of what we have found so far.

In Unit 4 we found that the basis of Christian ethics is to be found in the nature of God, and that gives us a starting point in our search for moral principles. The obvious, and arguably the most important, relevant feature of his nature is his love. As John puts it, 'God is love, and he who lives in love lives in God, and God is in him' (1 John 4:16). Love is his very being, so much so that 'He who does not love has not known God, for God is love' (1 John 4:8). It is a love that has been revealed in the most profound way, for 'God sent his only Son into the world that we might live through him … he sent his Son as the means of taking away our sins' (1 John 4:9,10).

Just as a triangle has three angles and would not be a triangle without them, so God is love. It is the essential characteristic by which he is known and reveals himself among us. It is because of who he is that we are called to love one another. It is a call to show the same characteristic as God in our human relationships (1 John 4:11,12). So we have identified love as a basic principle.

God

|

Love

From the God who is love, we can begin to build our moral principles by asking what love entails. We have recognised the need to recognise that love is not a sentimental compliance with everything that anyone wants. The wise parent acts in love, but not in a way in which a child gets everything it wants. Love has its

boundaries and recognises that the well-being of its object, which is its business, may need checks. In Christian ethics, the most important check is justice, which is simply the realistic face of love, so that to act in real love means that we act justly.

We now have the nature of God as the foundation of our moral beliefs and deeds, and two basic principles.

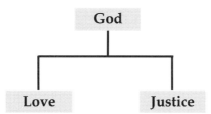

Yet we have also seen that love and justice can be difficult principles to apply because they are so abstract. In practice we translate them into more manageable principles which help to give them substance and identify the areas of our lives in which they operate. It is difficult to come up with a definitive list, but it is unnecessary, as well as being unhelpful, to try to fix the list too firmly. This is where other principles, which we have mentioned in passing, have their place. They express the way in which our love and our concern to be just show themselves. For example, we respect other people's property. We believe it is an act of love to protect the sanctity of marriage. We recognise the sanctity and dignity of human life, as an act of love for another. Both love and justice require that we respect a person's right to some measure of control of their lives, for example in the kind of things they do with their bodies. What we call human rights are important if we are to see justice done in the world, and we need to defend then. In general, love and justice entail that we respect persons.

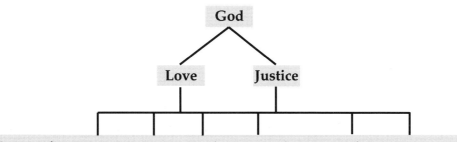

APPLYING OUR GUIDELINES IN THE REAL WORLD

Using these more specific principles in order to express love and justice, begins to give us some more specific guidelines to use in making moral judgements. But are they sufficient? How do we apply them to the real world in which decisions have to be taken?

It could be that we simply use our own judgement without reference to anything else. There may be times when we meet completely new situations and have to make an instant decision, and in that situation we may simply have to get on with it. If we want to take the decision making seriously, we may use various aids. For example, many of us turn to our Bible to see what light scripture throws on the matter. Our attitudes to some issues may be formed by the people around us, or by the approach that our church takes, and these are helpful guides to us. We may listen to what our conscience says. In some cases a particular course of action may seem obviously so right that it would be a travesty of justice to deny it, even we cannot find chapter and verse to support it. Then we have various examples around us. We may ask what Jesus would do, or picture someone from our past who embodied a Christian attitude for us. On occasions the most important consideration is to ask what the outcome of our actions will be. A hard look at the facts involved may also lead us to one course of action rather than another. Had they been other than what they are then we would decide in a different way, but they are as they are, and that helps us make our decision. Whatever we like to think is the source of our decisions, in practice most of us draw on a variety of aids which experience tells us will help us.

We are now in a position to to put together a picture of moral decision making, leading from the nature of God to basic irreducible principles which are expressed in further, more specific principles which we use in everyday life. To help us apply them, we take advantage of a variety of aids. So the picture is:

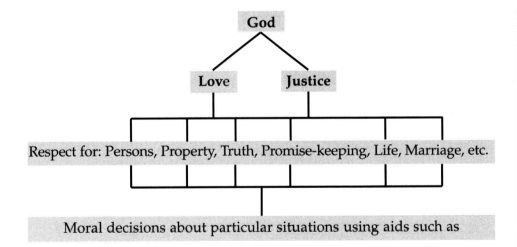

Respect for: Persons, Property, Truth, Promise-keeping, Life, Marriage, etc.

Moral decisions about particular situations using aids such as

Conscience

The Bible

Tradition

Consequences

Facts

ACTIVITY

Make a list of some of the things which you think you ought to respect in the lives of each of the following:

(a) an elderly person;
(b) someone with whom you have a close relationship, either at home or at work;
(c) a child.

Each of the lists is started for you with a suggestion. If you think it inappropriate, please feel free to reject it. Are there any further aspects of their lives you ought to respet?

(a) the elderly person
    Respect for dignity
(b) someone who is close to you
    Respect for privacy
(c) a child
    Respect for their right to have opinions

Unit 8 **THE NITTY-GRITTY**

OBJECTIVES

When you have completed this unit you should be able to:

- *Appreciate the role of different factors in moral life*

- *Appreciate the intellectual and cultural constraints on your moral decisions*

- *Understand why people have different ideas about what is right and wrong.*

When the communist regime in East Germany was nearing its end, it became possible to cross the border into Hungary and from there into the West. The iron curtain could be breached and many East Germans took advantage of the opportunity to leave. But some had a problem. They were well able to make the journey and they believed they would get work in the West, but they feared the consequences for their country of a mass exodus, particularly of professional people such as doctors. Some decided to leave and some decided to stay. It was a new situation and there were no clear guidelines for them to follow, so they had to make their own decisions. If they wished they could have talked of love and justice and the need to preserve life and human dignity, but at the end of the day they had to translate all that into their situation at their time.

"FROM HERE ON IN IT'S UNCHARTED TERRITORY."

That is what we should expect, for one of the features of principles is that, rather than prescribe that this or that must be done, they point us in the right general direction. A political party may have certain principles, but this does not mean that they will automatically do certain things when they are in power. For example, a general belief that a government should intervene in the lives of its citizens, does not in

58

itself specify *how* that will be done. In the same way the principle that justice should be pursued does not result in the same practices in every country. The principle that the love of God should be made known does not result in the same emphases or methods in every church.

If it is true that principles do not always prescribe a given course of action, and if we say that the ethics we find in the Bible are based on principles, then we should expect to find that the same thing applying there too. For example, if we apply the principle of the right to life to the abortion debate, we should not be surprised to find that those in different camps can agree that the principle is important, but differ in the way they apply it. If a continued pregnancy may threaten the life of a woman, some apply the principle to the woman and advocate abortion and others apply the same principle to the foetus and reject an abortion. But they work with the same principle. Principles still have to be *interpreted* in our particular situation, and decisions have to be made.

Decisions have to be taken in other cases where we know what we usually say, but it seems that our usual standards do not meet this particular situation. For example, we may believe that it is morally wrong to carry out the death penalty on offenders, but every now and then we meet a case in which there has been the wanton, ferocious killing of a number of young children. It may touch our emotions to such an extent that we say things like, 'I do not normally agree with hanging, but that person deserves to die'. These are situations in which our normal standards of right and wrong simply do not seem to apply.

Then there are other cases where there is a well-established response to a situation which we have never had to face up to. This is the case where a person has recently joined the church and wants to know what the Christian attitude is to legal separation.

In the hard reality of a complex world we have to decide what is the right thing to do or think, and this is where we begin to consider those factors that will help us come to an answer.

However, we ought to remember that most of us do not sit down and ask, 'What kind of considerations do I need to bear in mind here?' Neither do we go on and say, 'How do they apply to this case that is before me? For most of us, decision making is much more instinctive than that. We see a situation that is new and recognise what we take to be the relevant approach without conscious analysis.

In some cases, though, there are moral decisions which will affect the lives of many people, and sometimes those responsible for taking them are to give an explanation of their decision to society at large. This occurred when the Human Fertilisation and Embryology Authority recommended that doctors ought not to be allowed to use human eggs from aborted foetuses in fertility treatment, but that they can be used for research purposes. Their report contained reasons why they came to this conclusion.

Whether the decision is a conscious one derived from a considered use of moral theory, or one that emerges from instinct or experience, there are a number of factors that may come into play and which help us. It is to these factors that we turn in this unit.

CONSCIENCE

In Disney's film *Pinocchio*, the puppet is told, 'Let Conscience Be Your Guide'. As a rough guide to what is morally right and wrong, it has been a wise piece of advice for centuries. It was known to Paul, who advised the Romans that the Gentiles, who do not have the law of God, 'show that the requirements of the law are written on their hearts, their conscience also bearing witness, and their thoughts now accusing, now even defending them'.

It is hard to believe that there is anyone who does not know what it feels like to have a conscience. It is a feeling of pain that we get when we do something we realise or know is morally wrong, and often we feel we should not have done it. Yet it is not a judge. It is more like a counsel for the prosecution.

But it is more than that. There are also times when we face a possible action but we draw back because there is something inside us that says, 'This is wrong'. In these cases our conscience acts as a warning that there is moral danger ahead of us. It is a form of our moral consciousness. Paul adds a further case, and this is the situation where we speak of having a clear conscience when we have acted and have the confidence that we have done the right thing.

MORTAL
DANGER
AHEAD

60

In all three cases it is as though we come up against an inner self which reminds us that we are subject to a moral dimension to our lives, in the one case by accusing us, in the second by warning us that there are moral demands upon us, and in the third by approving of what we have done.

It is as though our conscience is an inner partner who approves of us or confronts us, and as such it is sometimes described as the inner voice of God giving us natural moral guidance. The description claims too much, because unfortunately our conscience can play us false. The reason is that our individual conscience is not ready-made, but is *formed* by all kinds of influences. For example, far from our conscience determining what is right or wrong, it is itself determined by what we learn of right and wrong from other sources. If we have been taught a particular set of values, then they will be reflected back to us as our conscience does its work. This is the reason why people in different cultures may have different consciences about their way of life. If I have been taught that cannibalism is morally good, then my conscience would not trouble me if I practice it. On the other hand, if I have been taught repeatedly that disobeying my parents is morally wrong, then I may well have a heightened conscience about the way I respond to them.

This explains why new Christians sometimes have no conscience about the things they do, while the rest of the church is very sensitive to them. They do not have the same background values on which conscience feeds. It also explains why we can talk about weak consciences or partially-developed consciences. In both cases, it occurs because there is a lack of knowledge and understanding and discernment about moral values. Our conscience, then, is dependent upon *how we feed our minds and spirits*; where it is fed on the ways of God and his beauty, there will be consciences which will guide us in those ways.

Because it does not automatically take a fixed stance on matters of right and wrong, conscience can be manipulated. We may use it as a safety mechanism that tells us that we should not do something, ostensibly because it is morally wrong, but in reality because we cannot cope with the matter. Or we may tell ourselves that what is really a matter of prejudice or self-interest, is the voice of conscience. Or again, we may repress it and refuse to listen to it. Those who regularly do morally wrong acts may initially have a conscience, but if they persist they will find that after a time it ceases to trouble them. It all arises from the nature of conscience as something which is formed in us in different ways and with different intensity, depending on how it is fed and what it is fed by.

TO THINK ABOUT…

Look back over the past few years and try to identify any things that you used to have a conscience about, but no longer have in the same measure. Alternatively, identify any thing about which you did not have a conscience before, but now do. In the light of this section on conscience, think about the reasons for the change.

Do you think it is:

(a) *A change in your beliefs which have strengthened or weakened your conscience on that matter?*

(b) *Personal interests which have dulled your conscience?*

(c) *Previous ignorance of some important facts or ideas which caused you to have the conscience you did, but which has now been remedied?*

The outcome of all this is that whilst our conscience may indeed be a vital way in which we know moral right from wrong, and that should lead us to accept it with respect, we also need to understand that it is not a totally reliable guide, and we need to treat it with a certain amount of healthy scepticism.

Although our consciences may sometimes let us down, there are some guidelines we can use to help us if we even suspect that our consciences may be giving us an incorrect message. We can check with someone we respect as being wise, know what they are talking about, and understand us and the situation. We can take note whether we are prepared to look at the details of our actions, or only generalise about the theory of it or look at the outcome of what we do. When there is doubt, we need to be examining the detail of what our actions entail, rather than salving our conscience with general high-sounding ideas. Finally, we need to recognise that our conscience is based on our beliefs and not on our emotions, and that truth is worth bearing in mind.

THE BIBLE

The Bible has a special place in the life of Christians. The Christian Church believes that in some sense or other, and it is not agreed on what that is, the Bible is the authoritative account of what God has revealed to human beings about himself and his ways. It reveals to us the God who is worthy of worship because he is the supreme being who is not dependent upon our created state, but is himself the Creator. He loves us to the extent of making himself a man and being offered as a sacrifice for sin. He has first-hand experience of what it means to be human, and he has experienced the kinds of pressures and temptations, joys and hopes that we have, and in it all he is concerned about the quality of life that we lead. All this is shown in his revelation.

As part of that concern, we believe that in the Bible God has things to say to help us form our moral values. Some Christians believe he has given us a moral rule book, and they look for texts which they can use to direct their lives. Others use it as a map to guide them over the moral terrain.

When we were thinking about the way in which Christian ethics may work, we found that it is biblical to think in terms of principles for living, and that tells us something about the way in which we ought to think of using the Bible. We need to look for those guiding principles and ask what they have to say to our situation at this time.

That is not always easy to determine, for two reasons. One is that it may be hard to know what biblical teaching and biblical incidents are about. We can read them and understand what the words say, but we do not always know what we are meant to take from them – sometimes because the Bible is largely a story of the lives and experiences of people and needs interpretation, and sometimes because it was written in a particular cultural setting at a particular time. The meaning of scripture is not just there to be read off from the words in front of us. The second reason is that even when we know what the moral truth of the passage is, we do not know what it means for our present situation. In other words, how does the guidance of scripture apply in our time and situation?

ACTIVITY

Think of the last paragraph as you read John 13:1–11. It is a straightforward story about a custom of Jesus' time. It is not obvious just what it says for our lives, if anything. What do you think its significance is for us? Is it telling us anything that we should do? Do you think it implies that we ought to wash each others' feet? Is there any moral truth here? Although you may be clear about what it has to say to you, perhaps now you can

The Bible does more than provide us with moral principles though. We need some guidance as to what principles such as love and justice mean in practice, and the Bible has a very specific part to play in showing that. In the events it records, it gives examples of how love and justice are worked out, and of ways in which they are abused. It also provides us with teaching which outlines what it is like to be the people of God who are called to a life of love and justice.

ACTIVITY

Read the following passages as examples of illustrative events or teaching. Briefly, write what you think they are saying or illustrating about living in love and justice.

> *1 Samuel 26:6–12*
> *Amos 8:4–6*
> *Matthew 5–7*
> *Luke 15:11–32*
> *John 8:1–11*
> *Philippians 2:1–11*

Yet it has a still wider role than just giving us moral principles and illustrating and teaching what it is to be committed to moral life. It shapes our thinking by giving us a general perspective on the world in which we live. From it we learn not just the revealed mind of God, we can recognise what God is like. As we read the stories of what happened to men and women all those years ago, we will begin to see the mind and heart of God and recognise not just his compassion and love, but his attitude to life in our world. We will appreciate something which is not reducible to a list of principles, but is akin to the knowledge we have of someone close to us, which words cannot adequately or totally convey.

Pre-eminently we experience this as our love for Jesus Christ grows, but it is there in the Old Testament where we see God with his people in this world. It is the soaking up of this revelation until it becomes part of us, more than the application of a set of rules or a list of principles, that gives us a *feel* for the way in which God would have his people live.

In the terms we have been using, recognising the truth of this takes us to the very heart of Christian ethics as opposed to any other account of ethics. We are invited to live, not so much as befits members of God's family, but as people who express who we are as those made in God's image and living with him in his world.

It is the Bible that is the source of that understanding and knowledge of the mind and heart of God, and it is for that reason that the Bible has such a vital role in forming our moral life.

TRADITION

ACTIVITY

Look at Mark 7:1–9. Look in particular at vv. 7 and 9 and write down what you think are two of the dangers, for Christian living, of following a religious tradition.

Now read v. 8 and think about the following two situations.

(a) The marriage of two members of a certain church was under great stress, and eventually the wife regretfully left her husband, though not at his wish. It was a very distressing time, but she moved away from the area, and after getting a divorce married another Christian. After some time she and her husband began to meet and make friends with her first husband. When the church heard that she had applied for a job with a Christian organisation, they wrote to the organisation concerned and to the couple to say that they thought there ought to be more repentance before she was employed in Christian work.

(b) A Christian family were on holiday in Bed and Breakfast accommodation, and on Sunday morning went to the local

65

church. They were made welcome and in the course of a conversation after the service, they asked if anyone could recommend a restaurant where they could get lunch. There was silence and then someone said that as a church they did not believe it right for Christians to use restaurants on a Sunday.

Do you think these are examples of commands or traditions?

Even with new churches, it does not take long to acquire some traditions. Our particular set of beliefs become part of our tradition, which we acknowledge when we say that we are 'an evangelical church' or 'a radical church' or 'a charismatic church'. Tradition is there when we say that we are Baptists or Methodists or in a House Church or that we are Anglicans. In each case we accept that we are in a tradition which has roots, and a history that gives us a sense of belonging. Arising from that, we may have traditions which dictate the way we worship, and some of us may find it difficult to cope when a new minister arrives and immediately makes us feel that our tradition is faulty or outdated.

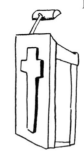

"I KNOW THE CHURCH HAS A TRADITION OF BURNING HERETICS, I'M JUST NOT CONVINCED IT'S THE SOLUTION IN THIS CASE."

Yet much as we like our traditions, experience suggests that if we are not careful, they can be a hindrance rather than a help, and this was the case with the Pharisees. Like Jesus, they were brought up in the traditions of the Jews, which had developed over centuries. Look again at Mark 7:4–9 and see how their tradition set their priorities. Notice v. 5, '"Why don't your disciples live according to the tradition of the elders instead of eating their food with 'unclean' hands?"' In reply Jesus quoted from Isaiah, 'These people honour me with their lips, but their hearts are far from me.' In Jesus' eyes, tradition actually took them away from God, by replacing the God who loves people with one who was to be appeased by observance of traditions.

There is another danger that applies to Christian ethics, and that can be seen in what we now regard as inappropriate or unnecessary traditions

66

of the past. In the early church there was a movement which sought to embrace the Jewish tradition of accepting Gentiles as converts to the Jewish religion. On this basis it was thought that the tradition of requiring Gentiles to be circumcised should be carried over to the Christian community, and it was something that Paul had to speak out against. It may have been an appropriate tradition for Jewish thinking, but it was inappropriate for Christians.

Another example is the tradition of evangelical groups in the 1940s and 1950s within which women used the minimum of make-up, and men were expected to wear their Sunday best to church. Many Christian groups have found such traditions unnecessary in the 1990s.

A third danger, highlighted by the Pharisaic use of tradition, is that tradition can become rigid and take on an authority all its own. A modern parallel is the way in which churches take entrenched positions on the form of worship they use, and reject alternative practices absolutely, often in a desire to preserve what they perceive to be the truth of the gospel. The point is not that we have different views, but that those views become set in stone, so that we no longer seek to understand or to ask questions about alternatives.

So far we have been discussing the possible effects of church traditions, but there are times when those traditions are affected by the non-Christian community and the traditions which are at work there.

Whether or not we agree with the way in which the Christian community now generally views the role of women in the church and in marriage, there certainly has been general discussion and change, and the tradition previously followed has in part been replaced by a less restrictive view. This has not come about because a group of Christians had a new look at scripture and found that their previous ideas were misplaced. Initially it came about because the general society of which we are a part became aware of what were seen as injustices and anomalies in the way in which women were treated. It was in this context that Christians went back to scripture to examine their traditions about the role of women. The result has been a new look at the matter, in the light of the insights that came from a feminist perspective.

This particular example is helpful because it presents us with two reminders:

- We need to recognise that whatever we say about this particular issue, in the course of time traditions do *change*.

- It may be that our traditions need *reinterpreting*. This is not the same as saying that they need changing, but that we may need to rethink what they are actually all about.

ACTIVITY

Give some thought to the last paragraph and, if possible, find someone with whom you can discuss it. You may like to use the following questions as a guide.

(a) Do you think that, as a general rule, the church ought to ignore or support changing ideas in the wider community?

(b) Some Christians hold that there are many areas of life where it is right to listen to ideas from non-Christian sources, but that there are one or two aspects of moral life about which the church must never change its traditional teaching. Do you agree and can you think of any such aspects?

(c) What moral values do you think are changing in our society?

(d) Do you believe they should be supported as being in harmony with Christian ideas?

Whatever their limitations and dangers, our traditions are important to us. They may need changing or re-stating, but they are helpful to us in three ways:

- They give us a continuity with the past which helps us to make our decisions in the context of the wisdom and understanding of previous generations. In few cases are we the first generation to have to grapple with a particular moral issue, and it would be foolish and arrogant to think that we are so much more informed and competent in handling it than previous generations. The continuity with the past is important.

- They help us to withstand and counter the more doubtful ideas that some groups who claim to be Christian come up with. For example, it is alleged that the Children of God encouraged Christian women in prostitution in order to gain converts. Our tradition is just one of the factors that prompts us to stop and question such a thing.

- They enable us to gain some idea of what the majority of Christians over a period of time have believed to be God's mind on particular issues. We are not alone in seeking to know the mind of God in our attempts to please him.

CONSEQUENCES

You will remember that when we thought about Dana's dilemma, we had to face the fact that to build an ethic on the consequences of our actions presents some difficulties.  Having said that, though, we must also recognise that, however we do ethics, the possible consequences of what we do are important to us. It would be quite foolish to run our lives without any concern for the *outcome* of what we do, and that includes the moral decisions we take.

There are some obvious examples. Take a domestic situation. Suppose our teenage daughter wants to hitchhike 200 miles to see a friend. We may not want to restrict her unnecessarily, but in deciding whether we agree or not, we would think about the possible consequences of her action, with the dangers she could face, and we would want to know what could be done to make the journey safe. To take another example, it is irresponsible to sell arms to an aggressive state without first asking how they are to be used.

There is good biblical precedent for this interest in the consequences of what we do. In 1 Corinthians 8 Paul speaks about those who became Christians and believed, even after their conversion, that eating meat which had been offered to idols had religious significance. Paul supported those who claimed that it had no such significance, and taught that it made no difference to their acceptance by God. However, this did not mean that Christians could therefore do as they wished in this matter. Those with troubled consciences about such things had to be respected, and in order that their misguided consciences might not be reinforced, those Christians who realised the insignificance of sacrificed meat should take care not to be seen dining with friends in a heathen temple.

Christian behaviour should take account of what may *result*, even though the behaviour itself is innocent, and possible results should affect the decisions we take about what is a morally right or wrong thing to do in a given situation.

ACTIVITY

Read the following passages and ask yourself what significance they have for

(a) Christians with scruples about Sunday observance,

(b) People who hold very strong views either for or against the use of the gifts of the Spirit in worship.

Romans 14:1–4; 15:1–3
1 Corinthians 9:19–23
1 Corinthians 10:23, 24

Sometimes, deciding what the consequences will be can be difficult and we have to make the best informed guess that we can. With hindsight we may realise that we took the wrong decision, and regret the outcome, but decisions have to be made on the best estimate we have. At times an even bigger problem can arise when we can see more than one possible consequence, for then we have to decide which is the most significant in the situation.

Try to resolve the following dilemma.

Suppose that normally you use a local garage for any work that needs doing on your car, but you have the feeling that they are not as careful and professional as you would wish. Let us imagine that one of your fellow church members, who is a car mechanic, has been made redundant, and decides to start his own car repair business. You believe that as a Christian he can be trusted and will do the best he can for his customers. Will you give him your business?

If you do it will help him to get established, and you will help a fellow Christian at a time of need. That is one possible outcome.

But there is always another possibility, namely that he or his mechanics will do a bad job. What might that do to your relationship with him as a fellow Christian?

What would you do?

Decisions, decisions! But that is what ethics is all about.

Although it does not provide a foolproof way of deciding what we should do, a regard for the consequences of our actions is a useful aid for us as we try to decide what to do about specific cases, especially where the course of action is not clear. But even where we think it *is* clear and we know what we would *normally* do, a little thought about the effects of our normal actions may change what we do.

FACTS

Facts are important to us. If we are repairing a broken iron, it is important that we know that electricity can kill, and if we are to make the iron safe, we need to know something about electrical wiring. Unless we know a number of facts, we could be putting our own and other people's lives at risk. However, if we know at least the most important facts about electricity, we can take precautions and do things that will give us a safe iron. Facts can be important in making moral judgements too, and when we are thinking about moral dilemmas we need to have any, and ideally all, of the relevant information – including that which is factual.

As an example of the obvious need for facts, suppose we believe that one of the causes of divorce that makes it morally acceptable is immoral behaviour in the form of sexual impropriety. If a person seeks a divorce, the fact that there has been such impropriety helps us to decide on the morality of that person's intention to divorce their partner.

However, there are other kinds of facts that may be relevant. For example, one of the facts that we need to have when we discuss whether it is morally right to ban access to video nasties in our society, is the effect they have on people, and particularly on young children.

The relevance of these facts can take another form. If they have a dangerous effect, then maybe we have to accept that children under their influence are not morally responsible for what they do. In the James Bulger case, it was said that the boys convicted of causing James' death were influenced by a video which affected their behaviour. In deciding whether those two boys were morally as well as legally to blame, we need

"DON'T DO THIS AT HOME."

factual information about the effects of videos on young children.

A similar case is that of the influence of pornography. One of the criteria we could use to decide whether it is morally right to ban pornographic material from shops is the effect it has on people and their behaviour. To

71

decide what is the morally right thing to do, then, we need to have as much factual information as we can on its effects. We need the help of the sciences.

One of the consequences of the role of facts in making our moral judgements is that the view we take of what we do may change as our understanding of the relevant facts change. This has happened in the way we approach abortion. In mediaeval times, Thomas Aquinas, among others, taught that the soul is created by God, though not at conception. He thought it was at some later stage in the development of the foetus. Before that moment when the foetus became 'ensouled' with the moral worth of a person, whenever that was, the foetus was thought to have the same 'soul' as an animal, and for the first few days after conception it had the same 'soul' as a vegetable. However, our knowledge of genetics has shown us that genetic makeup is established at the time of conception. If we believe it is that individuality that gives us moral status, our changing knowledge has changed the view we take of the time when the unborn has the moral status of being a person, and that could affect our view on when, if at all, abortion is morally acceptable.

A note of warning needs to be sounded about the way in which we sometimes use facts. Although they have a role in our decision making, we need to be careful not to assume that because something is a fact, it is necessarily morally right. For example, in some business circles it may be accepted practice to make false expenses claims, and everyone may do it. But because it may be accepted practice and a fact of business life for some people, it is not necessarily a morally right practice. The fact that everyone does it, does not in itself make it right.

It is tempting to say that because there is a state of affairs, there is a particular course of action that we ought to follow. However, it is a further question as to what is morally right.

PART 3
DOING ETHICS

Unit 9 HARD CASES

OBJECTIVES

When you have completed this unit you should be able to:

- *Survey different ways of reconciling conflicting principles*

- *Appreciate the strengths and weaknesses of various approaches to the complexity of moral life*

- *Understand some of the ways in which biblical statements help us resolve conflicting principles*

- *Evaluate the relative importance of some moral principles.*

It is a truism that if we say that a Christian morality is based on the basic principles of love and justice, we still have to decide what they mean for our everyday lives. In the last few units, we have looked at some of the factors that help us put principles into practice. At various times in thinking about ethics, we have had to recognise that there are times when it is hard to follow our moral principles because there are other considerations that need to be taken into account. There are times when our principles seem to conflict with one another. We met examples of these hard cases in the first unit. John believed he ought to keep the law of the land and not drive over 70mph, yet to do so in his situation would have endangered his own and others' lives. Sophie had to relate her respect for life to the circumstances surrounding her pregnancy and her sense of her own dignity and self-worth, whilst Dana had the dilemma of deciding between the promotion of human dignity and well-being, and telling the truth.

Unfortunately that is the way moral life so often is. If it were a matter of the simple application of one rule or one principle to one situation, it would be relatively easy to respond to moral dilemmas. It is usually far more complicated than that.

For example, a belief in the sanctity of marriage, which denies divorce, can come up against a belief that it is morally wrong for a man to repeatedly physically abuse his wife. The international community all too often faces a conflict between the immorality of giving in to the blackmail of terrorists who hold hostages, and the immorality of leaving innocent people in captivity when resources are available to gain their release.

It is cases such as these that make facing life with a Christian ethic difficult at times. We may believe passionately in our principles, but how do we reconcile them when they appear to be at odds with one another?

RECONCILING CONFLICTING PRINCIPLES

It would be easy to ignore some of the facts of life and retreat into easy solutions, and this is done from time to time. As an example, think of the case of someone wanting to know if they have a fatal illness. A 'yes' would be more than they could handle at present. In most cases like these we feel we have good reasons for not being straight and honest with the people concerned, but that does not match our belief that we should tell the truth. One very unsatisfactory way of dealing with the problem is to remain silent, but that is no real solution as silence can sometimes say just as much as words.

Another way that is sometimes advocated is to deal with the *reasons* behind the problem. We could ask *why* the sick person cannot handle the thought of a fatal illness. We might ask why *we* believe they cannot cope with the truth. Having decided the causes of the problem, they could be dealt with and the truth can then be told. Whatever the validity of such an approach, it does not deal with the fact that most people want answers when they ask questions, not when we have changed the circumstances.

There is another view that claims that in some extreme cases, there are people who act in such a totally immoral and unacceptable way that they remove themselves from the rest of us, and we no longer have any obligation to behave in morally right ways towards them. This is an argument that is sometimes used to justify the way in which the Hebrew midwives lied to Pharaoh (Exodus 1:15–22). The thought is that Pharaoh's order to kill the babies put him beyond the women's moral obligation to tell the truth.

This idea may reflect the way we feel about people like that, but it suggests that at times we do not have to reflect the nature of our God – who recognises the worth and dignity of us all. It is also hard to reconcile it with our own moral obligation to love, which does not seem to have any kind of reservation about it.

The truth is that we can refuse to face the real issues with which people have to deal, but such evasions do not solve the problems involved in living in an honest way. Unfortunately, even though it is sometimes easier to avoid facing issues, the reality is that we need to take decisions about what to say when people want to know, not when we are ready.

DOING WHAT'S 'RIGHT' REGARDLESS OF THE CONSEQUENCES

There are some ways that Christians try to cope with these difficult cases that are more tenable. One approach is simply to do what is immediately right, so that even if telling the truth will lead to murder, the priority is on telling the truth. People who hold this view are likely to meet the objection that this will probably cause a death, by saying that God will honour the truth and ensure that the life is spared.

There are a number of ways of justifying this approach. We could say that it reflects our belief in the faithfulness of God and there is at least one scriptural example of this approach at work. In talking about Genesis 20, for example, it could be said that Sarah honoured God by accepting her husband's decision to deny that she was his wife. She was taken by King Abimelech but spared any harm by God's intervention in a dream to the King.

This approach starts from the worthy premise that sin is always to be avoided, and that irrespective of the consequences, a Christian must be faithful to God's commands. Sometimes it is also claimed that what happens to the body is not as important as what happens to the soul, and the soul is what is involved in such things as telling lies, respecting your husband, etc. This particular idea owes more to Greek philosophy than Christian theology, and could mean that murder which is done to the body is of less moral significance than a white lie. A Christian approach rejects a division between body and soul.

You may be attracted to this approach and it may help you to handle situations where principles conflict. It certainly helps us to feel reassured that God's will is being done and that we are exercising trust in him for the future. You should notice though, that although there may be biblical examples of this approach working, there are no grounds for thinking that God will always intervene and ensure that the anticipated evil does not take place. Indeed, experience suggests that there are times when events follow their expected course. This is a case of using a biblical incident without looking too closely at theological considerations. It has to be said, then, that there is no guarantee that a life will not be unjustly taken if the truth is told.

CHOOSING THE LESSER OF TWO EVILS

A second approach is probably more familiar and says that we should choose the lesser of the two evils. If the choice is between telling a lie and someone being killed, then telling a lie is a lesser evil than murder. Both are evils, and whatever choice we make we will do something that is morally wrong, but in this case one is markedly less so than the other. Usually those who follow this way of dealing with difficult situations will add that, even though we are responsible for doing wrong, whichever choice we make, God understands our difficulty and will forgive us.

Thinking in this way may enable us to maintain that lying and murder are morally wrong irrespective of the circumstances. It keeps some objectivity in our ethics, but at the cost of generating a sense of guilt in us. After all, talking about the lesser evil does not remove the fact that it is evil. We cannot say that doing what is evil is of God, for that is just not what God is like. So if we think it right to think about lesser evils, it is only right in that we have to make a choice and we think we make the right one. It is not morally right though. Nevertheless, choosing the lesser evil is a workable way of handling some of life's complexities.

CHOOSING THE HIGHER PRINCIPLE

There is a third approach which on the surface seems similar to the previous one but is in fact very different. We can describe this as 'choosing the higher principle'. There are some assumptions in this, the first of which is that we do have to face these difficult cases, that they are real, and usually there is no avoiding them without becoming unreal and dishonest ourselves. But the real strength of this way of viewing them is in the assumption that there are some principles which are more significant than others, and when we are applying the lesser principles, we may not be under the same obligation to do what is right in all circumstances. For example, there may be times when principles such as respecting truth-telling and respecting the property of others may need to be laid aside in the light of a higher principle. Take a moment to think of your own experiences and see if this idea of higher principles has been at work in your life.

This is not simply an arbitrary way of handling difficult situations, but there are grounds for thinking that this is a scriptural way of proceeding.

ACTIVITY

Read the following passages and notice the way in which they all seem to imply that there are some sins and virtues that matter more than others.

> *Matthew 5:21, 22*
> *Matthew 22:36–39*
> *1 Corinthians 13:13*

TO THINK ABOUT...

Let us assume that we agree it is an important moral principle that truth should be respected. Can you think of situations where you think that it is legitimate not to tell the truth? Possible examples may come from what we may say in the context of serious illness or in our relations with our children. See if you can remember situations where you thought it right not to tell the truth or where, on reflection, you did tell the truth but now think you made a mistake. Doing this exercise presupposes that you will be very honest about what you think!

There are some examples of this idea of higher principles at work in scripture. In Exodus 2:15–20 it tells of the king of Egypt who ordered two Hebrew midwives to kill the male children at birth, but they disobeyed. When asked why, they told a lie. This is a denial of the principle that we should respect the truth. We can understand their dilemma and the reason why they told a lie, but the interesting feature of the incident is that apparently as a consequence of the lie, v. 20 says, 'So God was good to the midwives.' It seems that God was good to them because they respected the sanctity of human life, even though it meant that they told a lie.

Respect for other people's property and the negative command not to steal may be another principle which, on occasion, we may think it right to set aside. You may find this a little harder to justify than a need to occasionally tell a lie, but consider the case of someone who has no money and no means of getting any, but has young children to feed. Is stealing a valid way to get food in that situation? The point is that there are cases where we may hold to a principle but where there are other valid considerations which may cause us to set it aside in the light of what we take to be a more important principle that also applies in that situation. If this is so, principles act as our presuppositions that we will seek to behave in certain ways, but they are not hard and fast laws that certain things ought to be done in all circumstances. There may be valid exceptions.

This is in harmony with Jesus' teaching. On one occasion he was taken to task because his disciples took the ears of grain on the Sabbath (Mark 2:23–28). The charge was that they were doing *what is unlawful on the Sabbath*. It was a charge that Jesus refuted because he disagreed with the Pharisaic interpretation of the law that said that the Sabbath day should be kept holy. In doing so he was certainly implying that there were a number of possible interpretations of the law on respecting the Sabbath. But he did more than that. To justify his disciples' actions he challenged the authority of that law when there were other issues involved. He answered the Pharisees, '"Have you never read what David did when he and his companions were in need and were hungry? He entered the house of God when Abiathar was high priest, and ate the Bread of the Presence, which only the priests can lawfully eat, and gave it to his companions also"' (Mark 2:23–28). The reference is to the law found in Leviticus 24:5. He justified David breaking the law because there was a need that was more important than law-keeping. It is sometimes said that this referred to the ceremonial rather than the moral law, but we need to notice that Jesus is speaking of the way in which law can be fenced in to mean one thing, when its purpose is to promote the good of people. He went on, '"The Sabbath was made for the sake of man, not man for the sake of the Sabbath."' So just as David was justified in breaking the law when there was a higher concern, so were the disciples in the matter of Sabbath-keeping.

The following Activities may help you to think further about this approach. Be sure to attempt them both.

There is a major question that this approach raises, and that is whether there are any principles which are so important that they cannot, in any circumstances, be made subordinate to any other principle.

So far we have thought about three general approaches:

- Doing what is right regardless of the outcomes

- Choosing the lesser of two evils

- Choosing the higher principle.

Before you go any further, review what you have learnt in this unit. Try to put out of your mind the views you have had in the past, and ask yourself which approach seems to you to be the most satisfactory, both as a practical proposition and as an expression of biblical teaching.

THE ROLE OF INTENTIONS

There is a fourth way of handling these conflicts of principle. So far, the approaches we have been thinking about have focused on the moral standing of things that are done. There is a further approach which acknowledges that in these cases, our *intentions* and *attitudes* are also important and should be taken into account.

Let us return to the person, let us call her Jane, who is seriously ill, yet we judge that she will be unable to cope with the news that she only has a short time to live. Before we visit her, we hear that she is going to ask us to tell her if her illness is fatal. Do we tell her the truth about her condition knowing the anguish it will cause?

We could justify our decision *not* to tell her by our good intention that she should have the fullest life possible for her, and by saying that sparing her the unpleasantness and pain of knowing the truth, justifies a lie. Or we could use the same appeal to intentions to justify giving an ambiguous answer that enables Jane to read into it what she wants to hear.

These two ways of enabling people to deal with these difficult cases both have a long history – and both have been justified by the good intentions of those who use them.

TO THINK ABOUT...

Before you read further, let us assume that our intentions towards Jane are good. How do you react to the prospect of lying or being deliberately ambiguous? Would you lie or be ambiguous when you met Jane? What does your answer say about the place of intentions in the way you make moral decisions?

So far we have thought of cases where there is a conflict of principle, but there is a further kind of case that can be difficult, and that is the one in which the action will have *both* a good effect *and* a bad effect.

An example is the effects of an amputation. An amputation is carried out because it will be to the benefit of the patient, but at the same time it will mean that the patient is unable to do what could previously be done. An attempt to offer guidance as to whether to do things which will have that double effect, says that if we are not to be held accountable for the bad effects, then four conditions need to be met:

1. The action, in our example, the amputation, should be good or at least morally neutral. This means that although there may be good and bad effects arising from a murder, because murder itself is morally bad, it cannot be justified by its effects. On the other hand an amputation is morally neutral.
2. In deciding to amputate, we must intend to produce the good result and not the bad one.
3. The bad effect must not come first so that out of that the good effect will arise. This means that this principle does not justify punishing someone with the intention that in years to come they will be better for it.
4. We have to weigh up the good and bad effects, and if we think the bad effects far outweigh the good for that person, we should not go ahead with the amputation.

These are not a series of checks which must be applied when we are facing a dilemma: to do that could lead to some strange decisions. Nevertheless, they do give us further guidance when we face difficult conflicting situations in which we may be unsure about what to do.

Unit 10 PUNISHING THE WRONGDOER

OBJECTIVES

When you have completed this unit you should be able to:

- *Appreciate the strengths and weaknesses of different ways of justifying punishment*

- *Understand the reasons we might use to guide the way in which people might be punished*

- *Appreciate the importance of justice as a guiding principle.*

So far we have been looking at different factors that may be involved when we make moral decisions, and we have seen something of the part they play in what can be a complicated process. We have also seen how the various considerations may relate to one another in a pattern which reflects a Christian basis and approach. It is not claimed that it is *the* Christian approach, but it is an approach which does justice to what seems to be a biblical account of ethics.

In these next three units we are going to think about three widely different moral questions that arise when we consider punishment, euthanasia, and cohabitation. The intention is not to have a comprehensive discussion of them, but simply to see how some of the factors we have already identified can play a part in the way we deal with the issues we face in life. Theories are fine and we need them, but we need to see them *in action*, and that is the aim of these chapters.

In handling these different questions we will find that there is no single ethical formula that we apply. Whatever factors we take into account in deciding moral right from wrong, the weighting we give them and the role they each play has to be decided in response to the moral questions that face us. Above all, we will find that Christian ethics is about taking decisions where answers are not always clear.

THE PROBLEM OF PUNISHMENT

The first question arises from what we take to be a need to punish people. It is a fact of life that people do things that society or individuals consider to be unacceptable. It may be exceeding the speed limit, or an act of murder, or a child disobeying its parent. Whether they are trivial or serious such actions all raise the question of what we should do in response. We could allow such misdemeanours to pass, and indeed there are times when we may think it best to turn a blind eye, but these are not the norm. Our rules, whether in society at large or in the home, are there so that we can have an ordered life and be protected from those who might do dangerous things. In the home, there is the added intention of teaching children that there are ordered ways of doing things and there are right and wrong ways of behaving.

So how do we react to this flouting of our rules? One way that we use in practice, is to *punish the offender*, by which we mean that someone in authority inflicts some form of unpleasantness because a wrong has been committed.

The moral question involved in this is whether we ought to deliberately inflict unpleasantness on our fellow human beings. The problem is stark in cases where the punishment entails physical suffering. How can we possibly justify deliberately hurting someone? To hurt someone we need not be physical. Hurt can also be inflicted by depriving the person of what they would normally have, or by causing them mental pain.

TO THINK ABOUT...

Before we go any further, think about this definition and ask yourself which parts would be missing if we were talking about revenge or about spite.

WEIGHING UP CONSEQUENCES

One way of justifying punishment is by using the idea of the consequences of an action. In the case of disobedient four-year-old Tim, we may say that unless we punish him he will never learn the difference between right and wrong. Or we could say that we need to punish him so that he will not do it again. Both of these justifications are familiar to parents and teachers, and there are adults who tell us that they learnt what is right because a parent was strict with them – by which they often mean that they were punished for their misdemeanours.

There are two possible arguments here. One is that punishment will reform Tim, so that having been shown the error of his ways he will not want to disobey again. The other is that he will be deterred from disobeying again because, rather like a conditioned pet, Tim will associate disobedient behaviour with unpleasantness, and hence it is intended that he will think twice before doing it again. A rather simplistic difference between reforming and deterring is that the reformed child will not want to offend again whilst the deterred child will want to offend but is put off by the expected consequences.

This is where our earlier discussion about justifications in terms of consequences is applicable. You may recall that we found that a weakness in this approach is that of *knowing if the consequences will actually come to pass*, and this is the problem here. Many a parent and teacher has punished a child so that he will not do it again, only to find that he *has* done it again.

It is not just the uncertainty about this that makes us stop and think. There are two other things that arise from this. If we justify hurting someone by saying that they will not do it again, and then they do, were *we* ever justified in doing it? Have we not inflicted unpleasantness without any justification? Of course one way round this is to say that we *intended* them not to transgress again, but this is to change the justification from deterring to intending that people will not behave in certain ways.

This 'intending' may be familiar from your schooldays when you may have met teachers who were thoroughly unpleasant, certainly when they first met your form, and gave a clear message that this unpleasantness was a sign that if you stepped out of line there was still worse to come.

The problem with this is that it seems so unfair that on the basis of our intentions, before we have done anything wrong, we are treated as though we have already offended – or at least as though we almost certainly will offend. This does not seem very fair when no one has done anything wrong.

If we let our imagination run a little, we can exaggerate this situation to make the point clearer. Suppose that from things like the social conditions in which Terry lives, his family background, his educational record, his employment record and his friends, we could predict that, sometime in the future, he will commit a fraud. To deter him, or even to reform him, we might want to use pain in order to condition him so that he will not do it. Can we really justify treating people in that way? Where is the justice in such a practice? Here, you will notice, we are introducing the concept of *justice* as a safeguard against what may be an abuse of inflicting unpleasantness.

The second thing that arises from the uncertainty of these justifications based on consequences, is that in order to deter we may find that we have to increase the pain that is involved. Tim may not be one of those children for whom a stern word or a disapproving look is sufficiently unpleasant to have the desired effect. He may be immune to what we think is an appropriate degree of punishment. This is one of the facts that has a bearing on this kind of situation. The temptation, when we have to deal with people like Tim, is to make the punishment more severe if that is what is needed to deter him, but here is a new difficulty for us, for how severe can a punishment be before it is out of proportion to the offence?

Here we go back again to more basic ideas in our model, and ask if it is not unjust to inflict heavy punishment for a slight offence. It is the reverse of the outrage that people feel when a judge gives a minimal sentence to a guilty rapist, or a dangerous driver who has killed a child. W S Gilbert's maxim about the punishment fitting the crime appeals to our sense of justice.

"SERVES HIM RIGHT FOR STEALING THAT SHEEP."

What we have done in these two arguments is to import the basic requirement of justice in order to protect Tim from the effects of the weakness of a justification based on the consequences of what we do. The consequences of punishing people is important to us, both because of the possible damage that can be done to those being punished, but also because of the danger that there may be people (e.g. those who work with children and young people) who will get personal gratification from hurting others, and abuse their authority to punish. So we have to take the consequences of punishment into account, remembering the possible effects on those who punish as well as those who are punished. Nevertheless, as a justification, the consequences do not, in themselves, give us a very strong justification.

We have thought mainly about efforts to deter Tim from repeating his disobedience, but if we use our desire to reform Tim as our justification, there is something further to notice. That is the assumption that punishment actually does reform people. It is an assumption about a fact, and for it to be a good justification we would need to get some factual information about the effects of punishment. Does it actually reform? Or does punishment make people sour and bitter?

There would probably be a problem in getting the facts. Suppose a man is released from prison certain that his offence was quite wrong and that his way of life must change. From being a hardened criminal he becomes a pillar of society, convinced that the way of crime is wrong. But what caused the change? Was it the experience of loosing his freedom or was it the influence of a prison visitor? What are the facts? It is difficult to know in this case, but it is an example of the importance of having all the relevant facts in helping us justify our decisions.

If we want to use a justification based on the consequences of punishment, then we need the idea of *justice* to be inserted somewhere, and we need to have access to *relevant* facts.

ACTIVITY

Before you read on, pause and think.

For a moment, put aside ideas of deterring or reforming an offender. Try to recall any time when you have punished someone, maybe your own equivalent of Tim! Or if you have never punished anyone, recall an occasion when you have been punished or when you have seen someone punished. Make a list of any arguments you have heard used or can think of, that could be used as a justification. You do not have to agree with them or think they are strong arguments. Simply list them.

PUNISHMENT AS RETRIBUTION

There is another approach though, and that is to see punishment as retribution. At heart punishment *is* retributive, as it is about doing something unpleasant because something unacceptable has been done. As long as the two events are seen as part of a whole event, that is retribution. So if Tim was told that because he had been disobedient he had to go to his room, then we are talking about retribution. It is implied in our definition of punishment, but that does not necessarily mean it is morally right to punish anyone.

One way of justifying punishment would be to go to the Bible and look at examples of punishment and decide if they form precedents for Tim's case. We could see if there is any teaching about bringing up children, and note what that is. We could also notice references in the Old Testament to 'an eye for an eye', though this would be a good example of the need to understand what the phrase actually means, rather than what it says. In the context of the day it was not taken literally, but was a statement that was meant to *limit* revenge. We would also need to see it in the context of Jesus' teaching, which gets behind the stark tit-for-tat suggestion, and recognise that because of the barbarism that it could entail if taken literally, (eg, what would the literal punishment for rape be like?), we need to think of the principle of making a relevant response, rather than copying the offence.

THE SUPREMACY OF JUSTICE

All these considerations would help to clear the way, but the major help comes from the idea of justice, with its underlying concern to protect the dignity of our humanity as made in the image of God. Not to punish in some cases may simply imply that Tim may not be responsible for what he did. But if he was responsible, then to punish him is to respect his status as a human being, who even as a four-year-old, is able to take some responsibility for his life. To allow him that responsibility is to love him, and to act as God acts in showing his love by giving us responsibility for our lives, even though we make a mess of them. What applies on a large scale with God and us human beings, also applies on a small scale with us and Tim.

> *ACTIVITY*
>
> *Compare the suggested argument based on human responsibility with the list of possible justifications you made earlier. Which do you think is the strongest justification? Do you think it is strong enough to justify inflicting unpleasantness on another human being? Or do you think punishment is never justified?*

Whatever you have just decided, let us assume that it is possible to find an argument that is strong enough to justify punishing Tim. We have said that a concern for the consequences of what we may do to Tim is important, but perhaps we can now see why. If we can justify exacting retribution for an offence, then we must take the consequences into account when we think of justifying the *kind* of punishment we use. For example we may want to use punishment as a sharp shock, in which case the type of punishment may be different to that we may want to use when we want to deter someone from wrongdoing in the future. We may justify the form of punishment by thinking about deterring or reforming offenders, but the decision to punish at all is made by using some idea of retribution.

There are various ways in which people have tried to justify retribution and many reasons why some want to reject it, but for our purposes the important thing is that we recognise the different components that go into making our decision.

TO THINK ABOUT...

See if you, and maybe a friend, can think through the following specific case.

Jane Smith-Brown is a wilful only child, whose mother is a single parent. Jane repeatedly bullies and ill-treats other five-year-olds. Her mother decides she cannot accept that kind of behaviour any more, and as Jane has taken no notice of her mother's warnings and reprimands, her mother reluctantly decides she ought to be punished. Yet deep down inside her, Mrs Smith-Brown is not sure whether it is morally right to hurt her daughter, so she comes to you for advice. She asks if it is right to do this to Jane, and how she should decide what to do. You may have a lot of practical advice for her, but more importantly for our purposes, what are the considerations that you would take into account in advising her on the moral issue she is facing?

Unit 11 DYING WELL

OBJECTIVES

When you have completed this unit you should be able to:

- *Appreciate some of the arguments used to justify euthanasia*

- *Evaluate your own views about euthanasia*

- *Understand the place of different considerations in forming opinions*

- *Identify the key elements in the euthanasia debate.*

There are a lot of ethical issues being raised in the practice of medicine. Some arise from the advances in research which make it possible for treatments to be given that a decade ago were impossible. Others are raised by the increased costs of new and more sophisticated treatments at a time when it is difficult to find the resources we would like to put into medicine. Then there are the constant ethical issues which follow from our recognition of the rights of patients.

The sorts of issues that surround birth and death impinge on us all, so for our next reflection we will think about the taking of life by euthanasia. It raises different points from those we found in our last section, but once again we will see that it is impossible to apply an easy formula or set of rules that will immediately resolve the issue. Like most moral problems, there are relevant though possibly conflicting considerations we need to think about. Although you may have positive ideas about this subject, remember that our objective is to think about the considerations that may be involved in arriving at those ideas.

We may have an instinctive feeling about something as emotive as helping someone to end their life, and sometimes we need to follow our instincts about such matters, and do our thinking afterwards. After all, that is probably how many of us face up to such issues. But we are concerned with the next stage at which we begin to think about it more carefully. Euthanasia is a matter about which some Christians may be uncertain about their instinctive reaction, and that is all right and understandable, but it also illustrates the fact that when it comes to particular cases, doing ethics can be complicated.

SETTING THE SCENE

There are a number of ways in which death might be promoted or allowed. There is the practice of allowing a person to die, even though it would be possible to keep them alive. Then we are aware of the problem of knowing when or if to withdraw life support. But in talking about euthanasia in this context, we are thinking about helping a person to end their life, or ending it for them at their request. We are not thinking about simply allowing someone to die, nor are we concerned about ending a life when the person concerned does not wish it. Our concern here is with helping someone have a 'good death', where that person wishes to die.

Our concerns here are typically about people like Mrs Thomas who has grown very frail and who can no longer control either her body or her way of life. Mrs Thomas is worn out and is tired of living. In her estimation her quality of life is so poor that there is simply nothing left but to wait for death. Arthur is in a different situation. He is in his fifties and his doctors can do no more to cure his disease. They tell him that his life-expectancy is short, though they say that as the disease develops and the pain increases, they will be able to do something to ease his pain. Arthur has been an active man and feels he wants to keep control of what happens to him, even when it comes to dying. In their respective circumstances, both Mrs Thomas and Arthur would dearly like to control the time of their death, and at the right time would like their life to be ended.

THE CASE FOR EUTHANASIA

The moral question is whether we ought to help people by ending their lives at the time of their choosing. If they choose to end life at their own hand, that is one thing, but ought we to end it for them, even at their request? At present it is illegal to end life on request, though there have been several attempts in the past to change that, and Bills have been brought before Parliament. Thus far they have been thrown out, but there is a strong lobby in favour of legalising it.

ACTIVITY

Before we go any further, to clarify your own ideas, think about Mrs Thomas for a few minutes and write down the reasons why you would or would not support her request that her life should be ended.

Whether your reasons were supporting or not supporting Mrs Thomas, look at them and write down (or explain to someone) how each reason expresses a basic concern to show love for her.

What reason came first on your list? What moral aids seem to be appropriate and helpful here, and what factors seem relevant?

You may have felt some sympathy for Mrs Thomas because you feel you could well have met her in your own family or in an old person's home. She is not unique in her situation or in her wishes, and we feel some understanding and compassion for her. That seems a very Christian attitude to have and entirely biblical, as does a desire to respect her desire for dignity in her closing years, and her wish to be able to choose. You will recall that a regard for our humanity and dignity is presupposed when we love people and treat them justly.

That sense of compassion though, also affects Mrs Thomas' family, and that poses the question of whether she should take account of the pain that may be caused them if she were to be helped to die. Compassion for *everyone* concerned often presents us with a dilemma, for compassion for one sometimes means pain for another. It may be that the family would be relieved if Mrs Thomas died and her obvious discomfort and suffering ended, but there could also be a deep sense of loss that some families would prefer to delay as long as possible. Who comes first then, when we think of compassion, and how is it best expressed? We could claim it is compassionate to help her die, but we could also say it is compassionate to keep her alive and maintain the best quality of life that we can in the circumstances.

Our Bibles also tell us something about the value of human life, and we have noticed the way in which love and justice issue in a respect for the sanctity of life. Yet over the years, rightly or wrongly, the Christian church has recognised that there may be times when the principle of the sanctity of life can be put aside. Examples are causing death in war or in capital punishment. We also applaud the sacrifice of people like Captain Oates who gave his life to try to save the rest of Scott's last expedition,

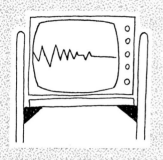

and Father Damien who gave his life caring for lepers. More pertinent is the recognition that there may be times to switch off life-support machines even though, technically, the person is still alive. In practice we treat the idea of the sanctity of life as a general and important principle to follow unless there are good grounds for setting it aside. Is this such a case?

> ## ACTIVITY
>
> *At this stage, do two things.*
>
> (a) *Notice how we are using the Bible in this discussion. We are thinking about its general theological teaching, rather than finding proof texts, and this will enable us to handle far more difficult ideas than a search for texts will.*
>
> (b) *If it is possible, in the light of our commitment to the principle of the sanctity of life, discuss with a friend any differences you can think of between switching off a life-support machine and euthanasia. Does our commitment to the sanctity of life help us in this case?*

Along with its concern for the value of human life, the Bible assumes the right of the individual to take responsibility for their lives. A Christian may say that such responsibility should be exercised in the context of God's values, and may not like what other people choose to do, but it is part of our human dignity that all of us have a God-given right to take that responsibility.

> ### TO THINK ABOUT…
>
> *Do you think this ought to extend to us being able to ask others to end our lives? Or does the principle of preserving life override any such thoughts?*

Thus far we have been raising some of the factors that argue for euthanasia: freedom of choice, compassion, human dignity and quality of life. They are all important presuppositions in the view of Christian ethics we have been considering, and as such cannot be dismissed lightly. Indeed they seem to be so important that if we are to reject euthanasia, we need arguments that are stronger.

THE CASE AGAINST EUTHANASIA

When we turn to the arguments that are thought to fit the bill, initially we can see that there are some facts that are important. For example, we know that Arthur has been told he has a terminal illness, and we have no reason to think the doctors' prognosis is wrong. Arthur's condition may even have been monitored by a computer, with the result that he is given very little chance of living much longer. However, there is always the possibility, however slight, that the doctors are wrong. There are enough people who say that they were told they only had a few years to live and yet have lived for years and years, for us to realise that prognosis is not an exact science. But if such mistakes can be made over people like Arthur, we have to ask if euthanasia is ever justified in such cases. Taking someone's life is an irretrievable act, but there may have been no need if the prognosis was wrong. It is one of those areas where medical science has taken us so far, but we need more certainty if we are to be sure we are doing the right thing.

If a possible error on the part of a doctor was the only consideration, we would have to weigh up whether the possibility that a life was deliberately ended on a mistaken prognosis, is a sufficient reason to prevent the practice of euthanasia for people like Arthur. You may want to say that even the possibility of there being *one* mistaken prognosis is sufficient to count against any taking of life. It is a 'safety first' policy that may be right, though it has to be placed against the pain and the wishes of the person concerned if their life is not ended as they wish.

As in so many ethical judgements, we have to decide between the risk of helping to take a life on a mistaken prognosis, and the amount of pain and suffering experienced by the Arthurs and Mrs Thomases of this world. It is an example of the difficulty of weighing our belief in a principle, in this case that of preserving a person's life, against the suffering of a number of people, in this case those who believe they have a case for wanting help to 'die well'. You may find it easy to decide which side to come down on, but remember that it is certainly not clear to everyone exactly what the answer should be.

A further way of arguing against euthanasia is by looking at the possible motives of those involved in the decision. For example, if it were legal, there are circumstances where it is conceivable that relatives may put pressure on Mrs Thomas and persuade her that it is for the good of the family for her to seek euthanasia – though the motives could be ease the burden of looking after her or to gain access to her savings. This possibility is one of the reasons why past attempts to draft a Bill legalising it have all tried to ensure protection from such pressure, and this is necessary if we are to respect the person's right to make a free choice, and make it a voluntary act. It is also partly why they have required that there be medical evidence that the prospects for the quality of life are as bad as thought.

We have already referred to the significance of respecting our humanity when we thought about some factors in favour of euthanasia, but it also presents us with a factor that may count against it. If the right to choose what happens to one's life is an important part of our humanity, then the idea of *voluntary* euthanasia is important. But how do we dec ide what is voluntary? Arthur may sign a form to say that when he reaches a certain level of pain or shows certain symptoms, then his life should be ended, and he may sign it voluntarily. But it may be that when the moment of truth comes he may want to retract, with his medical condition preventing him from making that known. If the request for euthanasia is made when pain is intense and life seems hopeless, are we in a position to say it is a voluntary request? In some cases it may be that a different treatment or new conditions may change the way things look, and make euthanasia seem an unreasonable proposition.

There is a further argument against euthanasia that has its roots in the Bible, and is derived from the idea that we have our worth because we are *persons*. This in turn comes from the revelation of God who as a person is Father, Son and Holy Spirit. The implication is that he is in relationship within the Trinity. The whole idea of having worth because we are persons, means that it is related to our relations which constitute our personhood. The conclusion we may want to draw is that as long as Mrs Thomas and Arthur are able to be in relation to other human beings, they are persons and as such their lives should be protected.

There are a lot of assumptions in this, but even so we may be attracted to the idea. It does not really help us make an argued case against euthanasia though, because Arthur could say that when he reaches the stage in his illness when he is unable to relate, then he would like to have his life ended. There is also the problem of switching off the machine which is keeping someone alive who is in a condition which means he cannot relate.

Our discussion has not been intended to present us with an answer to the question of whether we are morally justified in taking life. That is a much wider task than we can undertake in this study guide.

Rather, we have been introduced to some of the considerations which we need to take into account when we want to form an opinion. Our discussion has also highlighted a dilemma in the way we do ethics. In essence we have been looking at ways in which we decide how love is to be expressed for Mrs Thomas and Arthur, and whatever our own view, perhaps we have seen why we may not all come to the same conclusion – not least because of the people involved and their different situations.

TO THINK ABOUT...

Although we have been looking for arguments which will settle the morality of euthanasia for us, it may be that you will want to think further about the possibility that – within the very broad guidelines of respecting all those qualities of life and of our humanity that we have mentioned, and aware of the dangers that attend this matter – we need to be more flexible in our response to requests for euthanasia and acknowledge that what may be appropriate for Mrs Thomas may not be so for Arthur. May it be that the principles we have thought of are **guidelines** *rather than rules that decide that every case of euthanasia would be morally wrong?*

Unit 12 LIVING TOGETHER

OBJECTIVES

When you have completed this unit you should be able to:

- *Understand the biblical basis of marriage*
- *Appreciate the significance of cultural change for the way in which we evaluate moral issues*
- *Understand the significance of different factors we use in making moral decisions*
- *Examine the practice of cohabitation in the light of biblical principles.*

Charles and Janet have a problem. They have always believed that sexual relations outside marriage are morally wrong. Their son Tony is unmarried, but has been living with his girlfriend, Sarah, for over a year now, and they are coming to stay for the weekend. The problem Charles and Janet are grappling with is whether they should insist that their visitors have separate rooms, or recognise that they are living together as husband and wife and put them into the same room. Their problem is not unique to them, but is one that many others face as more and more people live together outside marriage.

In the past two decades, there has been a dramatic increase in the number of people in our society who are cohabiting. According to the Government Statistical Service, in the 1980s the proportion of single women cohabiting in Great Britain rose from 11.5% in 1981 to 26.4% in 1988. Among those women who married in the 1980s, there was a very significant rise in the number who, before marriage, lived with the man who became their husband. In 1972, 16% had lived with their future husband. In 1980 the figure had risen to 36% and in 1987 it was 53%. In other words, over half the women who married in that year had lived with their husband-to-be prior to their marriage. When we look at second marriages, it is

"THE SPARE BEDROOM'S THIS WAY."

estimated that approximately 70% are preceded by a period of cohabitation.

In recent years then, men and women have not simply been having sex prior to marriage, but have increasingly been living together as husband and wife without being legally married, and it is this dimension that highlights the moral question that we will look at in this unit. The question is, ought men and women outside a legal marriage live together and have a sexual relationship? This is the question that underlies Charles and Janet's difficulty.

BEHIND THE FACTS

The increase in the number of people who are cohabiting is a fact that we need to acknowledge, because it could be telling us a number of things. It could be saying something about the moral standards of our society, or about changing views about the role of marriage and/or sex in human experience. It could suggest that those who see the place of sex as being within marriage, have failed to make their case. It could just be that the Church has become dogmatic in its teaching and has failed to appreciate the significance of its traditional stance. As long as its views went unchallenged by the majority of the population, there was no need to look closer at what was really being said about human relationships, and that is a danger the Church always faces; but it may be that society in general no longer feels it has to comply with what the Church says, and is now showing a sharper insight into the nature and expression of human relations and of marriage, than the Church has traditionally shown.

These are some of the possible explanations of what is happening, though they are all conjecture. What is certain is that although cohabitation is becoming increasingly widespread and accepted within society, this does not mean that it is therefore morally right. Having said that, something significant seems to be happening, and we ought to take notice and listen to what is being said. The Christian Church needs to re-examine its position in the light of it, and not dismiss it as simply a wilful lowering of moral standards.

THE CHURCH'S VIEW

The Church has traditionally said that sex prior to marriage is morally wrong, and that position is unchanged. At the same time, normally we do not have any moral difficulty about men and women who live together for varying lengths of time, for reasons such as companionship or financial convenience, but who do not have a sexual relationship. Our stance on these two situations is reasonably straightforward.

Cohabitation is more complicated. One of the arguments that Christians have used in rejecting the practice of casual sex, has been the claim that for the fullest expression of its purposes, sex needs the context of a loving, stable relationship. It is said that without such a context, the sex act is diminished, and for this reason, among others, sex before marriage has been condemned as being morally wrong. The point of cohabitation, though, is that couples may have such a context, and be expressing a loving, caring, and committed relationship, even though they are not legally married. On the basis of that particular part of Christian teaching, sexual relations in that context ought to be morally acceptable to us. Some couples who are cohabiting, though not necessarily all, may have a better 'marriage' relationship than many who have legal married status. Yet undeniably, they have sex before legal marriage. One of the questions that cohabitation poses, then, is what makes sexual relations morally acceptable. Is it the context of a legally-recognised marriage, with its social acceptability, or the quality of the general relationship that two people express?

Cohabitation has become one of those areas of life where the practice of our society is inviting the church not just to face the fact that its traditional teaching is being increasingly disregarded, but to look again at what it *actually believes*, and to look behind the general moral assumptions of the past. Before we begin to think about that, you may find it helpful to think about your views about cohabitation, by reflecting on the following questions.

ACTIVITY

If you have been or were to be in the position of Charles and Janet, what would you do? At this stage, can you give your reasons for your reply? Write down your answers, so that you can return to them later.

The heart of the problem for Charles and Janet is what counts as marriage. If Tony and Sarah had been through one of the ceremonies we usually use a guide to marital status, there would be no problem, but they have yet to do that. Hence even though Tony and Sarah are living together as husband and wife, Charles and Jane are uncertain as to what to do. So the question is whether a marriage must involve some kind of legal ceremony. As a means of giving a social benchmark for marriage, it certainly does, but is there more to be said?

WHAT CONSTITUTES A MARRIAGE?

The first question we can ask to try to help Charles and Janet, is whether it is possible to have a marriage which has not had a legally-acceptable ceremony, and at the heart of that question we will have to ask what constitutes a marriage. Then following from that, if we were to decide that it is possible for there to be a marriage outside legal or religious ceremonies, we will have to ask if Tony and Sarah have such a marriage. The first question is the one that interests us.

In thinking about it, the Christian tradition is one source of help for us, and we have already noted this. However, there are also some background facts that may be of help. In the early days of the church, marriages were made on an informal basis, and it was only when Christian couples began to ask for the blessing of the priest that the idea of a Christian wedding began to emerge, though even then it tended to be held *after* the secular recognition of marriage. It is from those beginnings that the Christian tradition has set its own expectations and definitions of what marriage is and in Britain that has been given legal status. That has some positive effects. It affords the partners some protection if things do not work out, it gives some stability to society, and importantly, it recognises that marriage is part of the social structure of a society, and as such it is desirable that there be some form of social recognition. Clearly, the formal legal procedures that help define marriage have an important role in our society.

However, there have been other societies, going back before the advent of Christianity, who have had their own ways of recognising marriage, not all of which have been the kind of formal arrangements that the church and state have given us in the Western world. Nevertheless there have been other ways in which social recognition has been given to marriages, and this is something that we need to take into account in thinking about current trends.

In addition to the traditions of the Christian church and wider society, then, there is some factual information that will help Charles and Janet keep their thoughts in perspective when they think about Tony and

Sarah. It points to a felt need that is both long-standing and cross-cultural, that marriage requires some form of social recognition. It also suggests the possibility that there may be ways in which a society can give that recognition, which do not require the kind of ceremony that we have. Bearing that in mind, they may wonder if the increase in cohabitation is reflecting a change in the way in which social statements about the intentions of men and women who live together are being made. We may be in the process of a shift from the formal taking of vows, to a private act of commitment which is shown in the fact that people live together.

So far we have been reflecting on the relevance of some facts and of the Christian tradition, and although they have a large and important part to play in forming our opinions about cohabitation, this is an area where the major source of help for Christians is the Bible, which is very much concerned with human relationships.

BIBLICAL TEACHING

If we follow its teaching, we can rightly say that if two people are having a sexual relationship before marriage, then we describe it as fornication, and that is morally wrong. But we have been wondering whether cohabitation may be a form of marriage, and this is what we need to test, not only against our tradition, but also against biblical ideas.

> *ACTIVITY*
> *At this point look up Genesis 3:24 and make a note of the four criteria which describe what the church takes to be the biblical requirements for a marriage.*

If Charles and Janet were to challenge Tony about his relationship with Sarah and point to these four criteria, he may say that in their own minds, he and Sarah believe they meet them – and hence in biblical terms they are married, despite not having been through a legal or religious ceremony. He could claim that,

- They are monogamous.

- They have both left their father and mother, both physically and emotionally; even though there has not been a formal ceremony to witness to the fact, it is apparent for all to see in their openly living together.

- They are committed to what the Bible calls 'a man cleaving to his wife', by which Tony means that they intend to do what the word seems to have originally meant, namely 'sticking together'. They might say that they fully intend that the relationship will be permanent in the same sense that the marriage service refers to in the vows to *'have and to hold from this day forward; for better, for worse, for richer, for poorer, in sickness and in health, to love and to cherish, till death us do part'*. It was on this basis that Jesus spoke against divorce for inadequate reasons, and Tony may claim with some justification that their intention to make it a permanent relationship is every bit as strong as that of people who make promises in church.

- They have become 'one flesh', not only in consummating their relationship in sexual union, but in the wider sense of becoming genuine partners with a physical and emotional union in which they complement each other in forming a new unity of personality, support and purpose.

Criteria such as these have been difficult to interpret at times. For example, at different times people have thought that one or other of them is more important than the rest. At times it has been thought that a sexual union is the essential element in making the marriage formal, whilst at others it has been the cleaving together, with the sexual union having far less significance.

ACTIVITY
Look again at the features of a marriage mentioned in Genesis 2:24. Which do you think are absolutely essential for a marriage and which do you think are desirable but not essential? At this stage, try not to think about what is helpful in the day-to-day business of making a marriage work, but rather ask yourself whether, if any of these features were missing, it would still be a marriage. Tick the appropriate boxes:

	Essential	Desirable
Leaving the family home	☐	☐
Having a sexual relationship	☐	☐

Intending to stay together, if at all possible	☐	☐
Having a 'togetherness' which seeks the good of the partner	☐	☐

There are two warnings we need to heed at this stage.

1. We need to be careful not to be dogmatic in our views. There has been, and if you can compare your list of essentials with a friend you may find that there still is, a range of views on how we should understand the Bible on these matters. It is one of those cases we noted in an earlier chapter, when we thought of the problem of knowing what the biblical record *means*, as distinct from what it *says*.

2. Although Tony and Sarah may claim, with some justification, that because their relationship is built on love and commitment, it is as morally right as that of couples who have been through legal marriage ceremonies, no doubt there are other cohabiting couples who are unable to make that claim. For example, some couples may not be able to say that they intend to stay together, or they may say that they do not have or want any 'togetherness' in the sense of complementing one another. In a similar way there may also be couples who have been through a legal ceremony, who may say the same things.

ACTIVITY

Now we have to face the big question. In the light of what you know of Tony and Sarah, no doubt you will agree that in a legal sense they are unmarried, and in that case you may want to say they are guilty of fornication. But do you think they are married in a biblical sense?

In your view, should we make the same moral judgement about all couples who are cohabiting? May some be morally acceptable while others are not? The most important part of deciding these things, is the reasons that lead you to your opinion. Try to list them, and then ask yourself if they are strong, fair or poor reasons.

One of the differences Christians may have when deciding about these things, is in their views about the *purpose* of marriage. In today's world there is a genuine concern for meaning and value in relationships, which is a concern for the quality and the very soul of a relationship. It seeks a reality where words are matched by deeds, and there is a genuine and open meeting of two human beings, with commitment to a shared life. It may be that an increase in the divorce rate reflects the risks which this approach entails. If we need a shorthand way of describing it, we could use the word 'love' to characterise it, though in the sense of a self-giving to one another, and certainly not as a romantic indulgence.

On the other hand there is a more functional view that says that the essence of marriage is two people committing themselves to stay with one another and to support one another through life, even though the quality of the relationship may not be very good. In practice it makes more of the rituals of marriage, than the quality of relationships, and is reflected in the way in which the institution of marriage is sometimes defended at the cost of the people within it. A way of characterising this could be to say it is about seeing that each partner is treated justly, in that vows are kept and each partner sees to the well-being of the other. Using the words 'love' and 'justice' to characterise these two views is obviously an oversimplification of the positions being described, but the words convey something of the difference between the two positions, and that is what they are intended to do in this context.

ACTIVITY

If you can, you may find it helpful at this point to discuss with a friend which of these two views of marriage is closest to your own view. If you want to say that marriage is a combination of the two, which do you think most nearly represents what marriage should be about? Is that different to the view you would prefer?

When you have done this, read Matthew 12:9–14 and ask yourself if it has anything to say about your view of marriage.

Remember that the point of these case studies is to illustrate the way in which various principles which underlie Christian ethics have a part to play in our decision making. They are not meant to be exhaustive discussions, and we must recognise that in what is only a brief and limited discussion. However, having seen that the Christian and social traditions, some factual information, and the Bible, all have something to contribute, what views could we take about cohabitation? There seem to be three main possibilities:

1. We can say that we have to live within a society where it is still the *normal expectation* that marriage will begin with a ceremony, and that in view of the way that reflects the public acknowledgement of marital status and helps to regulate family life, cohabitation is morally wrong.

2. An alternative view will say that *an intention to meet biblical criteria for marriage* is sufficient for us to recognise that a particular cohabiting relationship could be morally right. It may be contrary to our traditional ideas, but we could argue that the quality of the relationship in a full commitment is the crucial factor. Any concern about the need for a public recognition of a marriage could be met by saying that cohabitation should be open and public, and that in itself will be the public statement of intent.

3. A third view will say that a cohabiting couple have an *embryonic marriage* which needs fostering and bringing to full term when it will be publicly acknowledged in a public ceremony. This is not to deny the moral rightness of the relationship where the intentions are that there will be a ceremony at some stage, and where the biblical criteria are met. As with the second option it recognises that there may be all the qualities of a marriage within a relationship, and it seeks to do justice to that, but also – like the second option – it means treating each couple separately, and making judgements about the morality of their relationship within the context of the developing story of their lives.

ACTIVITY

You may like to discuss these options with a friend and analyse their strengths and weaknesses. In the light of thinking about cohabitation, ask yourself what you think is the key feature of Christian ethics in deciding what is morally right for people who are cohabiting. Is it in the intentions of the couple? Is it in the outcome of cohabitation? Or is there something intrinsically right or wrong in cohabitation?

Earlier in the unit you were invited to write down what you would have done if you had to decide whether to put Tony and Sarah in separate rooms. Once again try to put yourself in the position of Charles and Janet. Look at your earlier answer and the reasons for it. In the light of your reading and thinking about the matter, would you still give the same answer? Try to say why.

CONCLUSION

This manual has not offered a theological discourse on ethics. We have been examining ways in which we might handle our moral life and, hopefully, exploring the ways in which we live, as well as our ideas and attitudes.

However, it is very important that we realise that moral life is not just about us as individuals. It is about you and me as members of wider communities such as our church, our village, our city, our world. As such we are shaped by them and in turn help to shape them by what we do and do not do. We are part of communities of people who form an ongoing chapter in a story of human beings who seek to do what is the best for themselves and for others within that wider context.

Ethics is not about personal choices made in isolation from others. It is a joint search with others for what life ought to be like in community, and in Christian ethics that community includes God. It means that although our efforts have been focused on moral decision making, there is far more to moral life than that.

Essentially, moral decisions are not attempts to deal with 'cases', though that is a convenient way of thinking about the problems involved. Our decisions are part of who and what we are as people, and part of the wider human story. What we do as a result of our approach to moral life is important, but it arises from what we are, the kind of people we are, the way we see God and respond to the people and world around us. It comes from the fullness of our own lives and the extent to which we are whole, integrated persons. They are about *us*, not about abstract rules which we understand and apply. We shape our situations, live with them and react to them, and what we are affects all that.

This makes sense in the context of what we have been looking at in this study guide. We have seen that love is the key to who God is and what he would have us do. But love is not a technique to be applied. It is the response of hearts that are safe in the knowledge of their own worth, and which can reach out to others for their good. That is primarily about what we *are*. What we *do* is a further question…

APPENDIX

BIBLIOGRAPHY AND FURTHER READING

Some of the following books are now out of print, but your local library should be able to obtain these for you.

Pastoral Ethics in Practice	David Atkinson	Monarch (1989)
The Moral Maze	David Cook	SPCK (1983)
The Quest for Christian Ethics	Ian Fairweather and James McDonald	The Handel Press (1984)

(This book contains a fuller discussion than the other books on this list.)

Dilemmas	Richard Higginson	Hodder and Stoughton (1988)
New Directions in Theology	Kevin Kelly	Geoffrey Chapman (1992)
Mere Morality	Lewis Swedes	Lion (1983)

Notes

Notes